The Care & Keeping of YOU 1

The #1 Body Book for Younger Girls

by Valorie Lee Schaefer
Cara Natterson, MD, medical consultant
illustrated by Josée Masse

American Girl

Dear American Girl,
I am a preteen, and all of a sudden growing up is becoming a big and important issue. I want to talk to my parents about it, but I don't know how. Please help me.

Growing Up

Published by American Girl Publishing

No part of this book may be used or reproduced in any manner whatsoever without written permission except in the case of brief quotations embodied in critical articles or reviews.

23 24 25 26 27 28 29 QP 10 9 8 7 6 5 4 3 2 1

Editorial Development: Michelle Nowadly Watkins, Andrea Weiss, Carrie Anton, Mary Richards Beaumont, Mel Hammond, Barbara Stretchberry
Creative Director: Kym Abrams
Managing Art Director: Marilyn Dawson
Design: Ingrid Hess, Camela Decaire, Jessica Rogers
Production: Caryl Boyer, Tami Heinz, Jodi Knueppel, Kristi Lively
Medical Consultants: Lia Gaggino, MD & Cara Natterson, MD

This book is not intended to replace the advice of or treatment by other health-care professionals. It should be considered an additional resource only. Questions and concerns about mental or physical health should always be discussed with a doctor or other health-care professional.

Library of Congress Cataloging-in-Publication Data

Names: Schaefer, Valorie Lee, author. | Natterson, Cara, 1970- consultant. | Masse, Josée, illustrator.
Title: The care & keeping of you. 1, The body book for younger girls / by Valorie Lee Schaefer ; Cara Natterson, MD, medical consultant ; illustrated by Josée Masse.
Other titles: Care and keeping of you
Description: Fourth edition. | Middleton, WI : American Girl Publishing, [2023] | Includes index. | Audience: Ages 8+
Identifiers: LCCN 2022051598 | ISBN 9781683372189 (paperback)
Subjects: LCSH: Girls--Health and hygiene--Juvenile literature. | Grooming for girls--Juvenile literature. | Preteens--Health and hygiene--Juvenile literature.
Classification: LCC RA777.25 .S333 2023 | DDC 646.7/046--dc23/eng/20221114
LC record available at https://lccn.loc.gov/2022051598

© 1998, 2012, 2018, 2023 American Girl. American Girl and associated trademarks are owned by American Girl, LLC. American Girl ainsi que les marques et designs y afférents appartiennent à American Girl, LLC. MADE IN CHINA. FABRIQUÉ EN CHINE. Retain this address for future reference: American Girl, 2330 Eagle Drive, Middleton, WI 53562, U.S.A. Conserver ces informations pour s'y référer en cas de besoin. American Girl Canada, 2330 Eagle Drive, Middleton, WI 53562, U.S.A. Manufactured, imported or distributed by: Mattel Europa B.V., Gondel 1, 1186 MJ Amstelveen, Nederland. Mattel U.K. Limited, The Porter Building, 1 Brunel Way, Slough SL1 1FQ, UK.

americangirl.com/service

Not all services are available in all countries.

MO

Letter to You

When you were little, your parents or other trusted adults took care of you. Now that you're older, you're taking over a lot of that responsibility, and it's not always easy to know what to do or how to ask for help.

You might be excited, or you might be embarrassed at times when you think about the changes ahead. That's totally normal!

So, what can you do? For starters, you need to get information. The more you know about your body, the less confusing and embarrassing growing up will seem— and the easier it will be to talk about.

We hope the head-to-toe advice in this book will give you the words to start a conversation with your parents or other adults you trust. They were there for you when you were little, and they can still be there for you now. If you speak up, no matter how awkward you feel, your confidence and spirit will grow right along with your body!

Your friends at American Girl

This book has been a trusted resource for girls since 1998. While much of the information and advice about growing up hasn't changed, some things have. This new edition brings you the best, most up-to-date advice for your changing body.

Contents

Body Basics
The Basic Facts   8

Heads Up
Hair Care   16
Hair Scare!   18
Ears   20
Eyes   22
Mouth   24
Braces   28
Face   30
Acne   32
Sun Sense   34
Body Talk   36

Reach
Hands   40
Underarms   42
Breasts   44
Bras   46
Body Talk   50

Belly Zone
Shapes & Sizes   54
Food   56
Nutrition   58
Body Talk   62

Big Changes
Pubic Area   66
Period   68
Body Talk   78

On the Go
Legs   82
Feet   84
Fitness   86
Sports Safety   88
Rest   90
Sleep Troubles   92
Body Talk   94

The Girl Inside
Your Feelings   98
The Whole You   102

9 YRS. —

7 YRS. —

5 YRS. —

3 YRS. —

1 YR. —

Body Basics

With your body on the brink of some pretty big **changes,** it's time to start taking control of your **health** and **well-being.** This section introduces you to the **basic facts** about **puberty** and reminds you to take care of yourself, inside and out.

The Basic Facts

Taking care of your body is a lifelong job. And it's more important than ever right now, while you're going through big changes.

Are you the shortest girl in your class, or do you tower above everyone? All of that could change in the very near future!

Calling ALL Bodies!
Everybody has a body. And every body is a good body. All bodies are welcome here. This book is for you!

The Changes Ahead
Puberty is a special time of growth and change. Everyone goes through it. It begins for most girls between the ages of 8 and 13, and it ends when your body has reached its adult height and size, around ages 15 to 17.

During puberty you'll grow up and out, and not all parts will grow at the same rate. At times you might look and feel like a puppy whose paws are too big for its body! You'll notice changes in your skin, hair, breasts, and other parts of your body. And you'll experience new emotions, too. All these changes are caused by hormones, chemicals your body produces to change you from a young girl to a woman.

Get Informed
You might be eager for your body to get growing, or you might be worried about the changes ahead. But the more you know about your body, the less surprised you'll be. So get the facts. Reading books like this one is a great start. You'll find answers to questions you may have never even thought of!

But no book is a substitute for talking to your parents, your doctor, or other trusted adults—people whose job it is to help take care of you. No question is too silly or too embarrassing to ask. Remember, the grown-ups in your life were once your age, and they have experience and wisdom to share with you.

Celebrate YOU

Remember that your body is a work in progress. Focus on all the unique things that make you YOU, and all the great things your body can do.

You may feel like you don't have any control over your growing body. Not true! You *are* the boss when it comes to taking care of these basics.

Pay Attention

Your body is talking to you. Can you hear it? Learn to tune in to your body and hear its warnings. If your body says it's thirsty, drink more water. If your body is tired, give it a rest. When you feel hungry, reach for a nourishing snack.

Keep Clean

All that hard work your body's doing to grow up means you'll need to bathe or shower more often, especially if you're active in sweaty sports.

Exercise

You don't have to be a star athlete to be healthy. Skateboard to a friend's house, dance to your favorite music, take your dog for a walk, or stretch out with some yoga. The more you move your body, the better you'll feel.

Just Don't

No girl can feel her best with nicotine, alcohol, or drugs in her body. Though drinking, vaping, and smoking might seem "grown-up," the truth is, they're bad for your health. And drugs can destroy your family and future. A smart girl turns her back and walks away from so-called friends who put pressure on her to "just try it."

PRIVATE

Your body is yours and yours alone. You have the right to protect it and keep it private from anyone—family, friend, or stranger. If any person touches you in a way that makes you feel uncomfortable, tell an adult you trust immediately. You should never keep a secret that is harmful to you or protect anyone who is hurting you.

If you feel good about yourself on the inside, you'll sparkle on the outside!

Most images of women you see on TV, in movies, or on social media just aren't realistic. Look around. Women's bodies come in all shapes and sizes and with differing abilities. There's no one type of body that's better than another. All bodies are good bodies!

Compare? No Fair!

It's tempting to compare yourself to the people you see on TV and in movies. But hold on! Is it fair to measure yourself against made-in-Hollywood images created by makeup artists and photo wizards? No way! You don't need to measure yourself against anyone at all, including friends or other girls at school. You're you—a one-of-a-kind original—and you're beautiful in your own unique way.

It Isn't a Race

A girl's body changes to a woman's body gradually, not overnight. Each girl develops at her own rate. Even sisters don't develop at the same rate. And it's important to remember that growing up isn't a race. There are no prizes for being the first—or last—girl to lose all her baby teeth or to wear a bra. Trust that your body will do all the right things at the time that is right for you.

What's on the Inside

The most interesting girl in the room isn't the one who wears the latest styles or has a certain look. It's the girl who brims with self-confidence. She's the one who stands head and shoulders above the crowd. That girl can be you. It all starts with a positive attitude.

To have a positive attitude, try to see yourself as a whole person shining through your features. Focus on what's best about you and refuse to hunt for negatives. Don't doubt yourself—be proud of yourself for doing your best.

Kindness Counts

As your body is growing and changing, be kind to yourself. And remember to be kind to other girls, too. There is never a good reason to comment on another's body. The very best thing you can say about anyone's body is nothing at all.

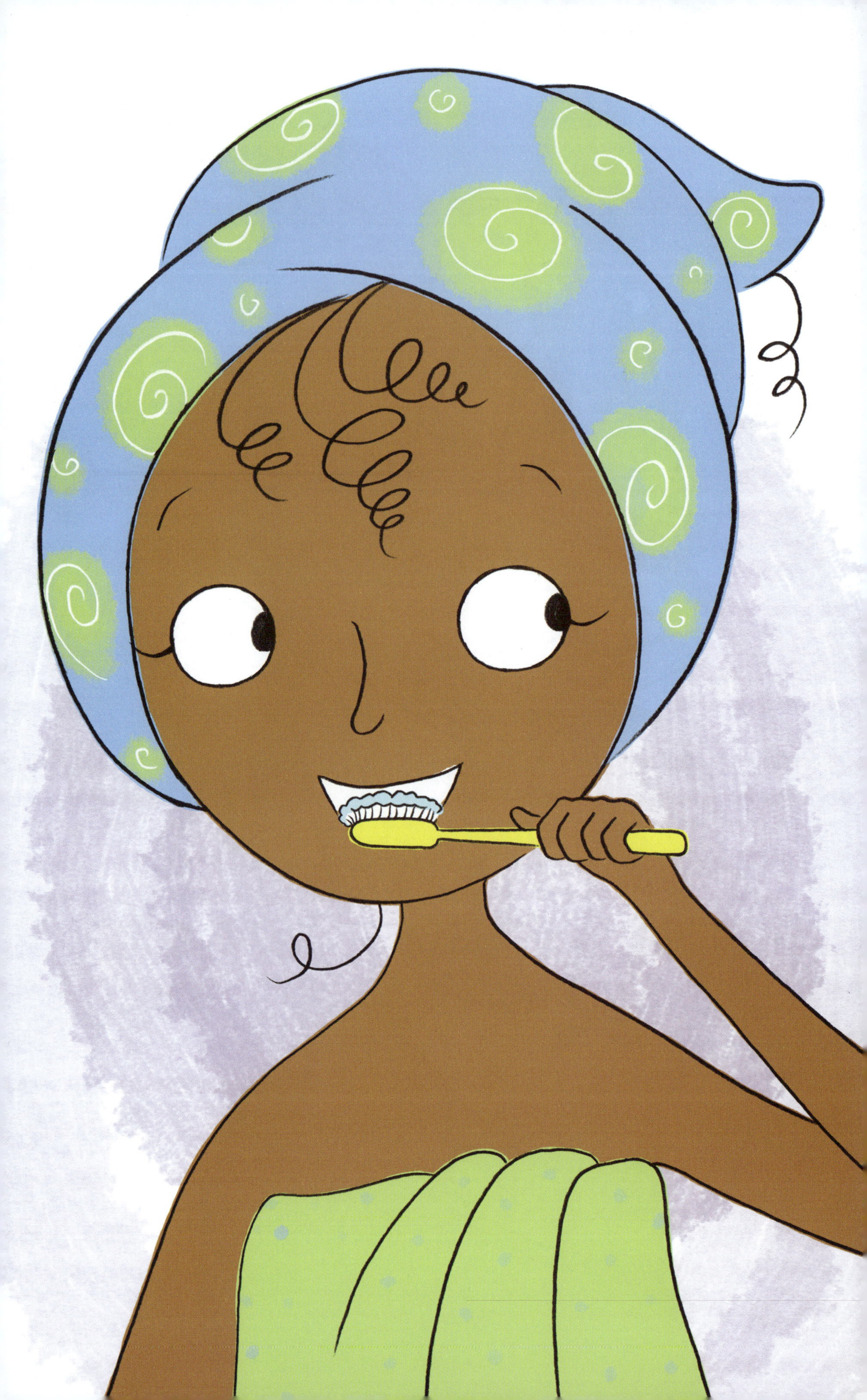

Heads Up

Let's take it from the top, with tips for handling your **hair,** sound advice on **ears,** and bright tips for bright **eyes.** Learn how a healthy **mouth** makes for a great grin. Brush up on tooth, gum, and **braces** basics. Finally, get the scoop on the skin you're in so you can put your best **face** forward!

Hair Care

Start your everyday grooming routine right at the top by taking care of your hair.

Do Know Your Hair Type

Choose a shampoo that's right for your type of hair. Some girls have thick, textured hair and some girls have finer, smoother hair. Most girls use some kind of conditioner on their hair to keep it soft and frizz-free. Conditioner can also help prevent tangles, especially if you have long hair. Ask your parents or hairstylist what kind of shampoo and conditioner works best for your type of hair.

Do De-chlorinate

If you're a swimmer, rinse the pool water out of your hair after every dip. Chlorine can be very drying, and other chemicals can turn blond hair green. You can buy special shampoos made for swimmers, but regular shampoo often works just as well.

Do Wash Tools

Make sure your brushes, picks, and combs are as squeaky clean as your hair. About once a week, give them a swish in warm, soapy water—you can use shampoo or even mild dish detergent. Rinse thoroughly.

Do Wash as Needed

Some girls might need to wash their hair every day, especially if they have oily hair, swim frequently, or sweat a lot in sports or other active hobbies. Other girls might only need to wash their hair a few times a week or even just a few times a month to keep hair from becoming dry or fragile.

Don't Mangle Tangles

While your hair is still wet, use a wide-tooth comb to detangle small sections. Start with the ends first and work your way up. If you hit a rough spot, don't yank! Gently work the comb through your hair. Girls with curly hair should only brush or comb their hair when it's wet. Girls with textured hair or girls with smooth, straight hair can comb when their hair is dry.

Do Use the Right Tools

Use tools that are made for your type of hair. If you have textured or curly hair, combing through your hair with just your fingers works great! Or you can use a wide-tooth hair pick. If you have straight or wavy hair, a bristled brush can detangle and smooth your hair. Ask other people with hair similar to yours what works best for them.

Don't Share

Sharing is a good thing, except when it comes to hair tools. Don't borrow from family members or friends, and don't lend them yours. It isn't stingy—it's good hygiene.

Don't Overheat

Blow-dryers, straightening irons, and curling irons can really dry out your hair. If possible, let your hair dry naturally. If you use a blow-dryer, use the warm or cool setting. Don't use straightening irons and curling irons every day—save them for special occasions.

Hair Scare!

When hair-raising horrors happen to you, here's how to handle them.

Getting Gum Out
Uh-oh! Somehow you've managed to get a big, sticky wad of gum in your hair. Before you reach for the scissors, try this age-old trick. Spread a glob of peanut butter on the gum. Work the peanut butter through your hair until the gum comes out. The peanut butter will wash out with a regular shampoo.

Greasy Hair

During puberty, your oil glands get more active. For some girls this means greasy hair. If the roots of your hair look oily almost every day, you might have to shampoo more often or change the type of shampoo you're using.

Dandruff

Does your scalp feel dry and itchy? Are your shoulders covered with flakes of skin, making your dark-colored shirts look like they're sprinkled with snow? You might have a case of *dandruff,* a very common condition that's easy to treat. Try a dandruff shampoo, and if that doesn't work, ask your doctor for something stronger.

Hair products such as mousse, sprays, styling creams, gels, and oils can cause flakes and itching from buildup. Shampoo regularly to remove the buildup.

EEK—a Louse!

Head lice are a common problem among schoolkids everywhere. These tiny wingless parasites thrive in thickets of human hair. They bite the scalp, leaving tiny sores that itch like crazy. Worst of all, a single louse can lay hundreds of eggs, called *nits,* right on your head! If lice are on the loose at your school, take action to protect yourself. Don't share combs and brushes with friends. Don't swap hats, hair bands, or headphones, and don't trade pillows at sleepovers.

If you suspect unwelcome guests on your head, see your doctor or school nurse. They know a louse when they see one. Live lice are small and gray and move around. Nits look like white grains of sand and are often found along the hairline above the neck and behind the ears. If it turns out you have lice, your parents can buy delousing products and follow the instructions carefully to get rid of the lice completely and to keep them from coming back.

Nits attach themselves to hair and can be hard to get out. A special fine-tooth "nit comb" can help pick out the nits.

Ears

Ears are easy to care for. They need just a little help from you to stay healthy inside and out—so every sound you hear will be crystal clear.

Squeaky Clean

Your ears get washed every time you shampoo or shower. In most cases, that's all the cleaning they need. Shake your head to remove excess water, and use a towel, washcloth, or cotton swab to wipe off the outer part of your ears. NEVER stick a pointy object into your ears—not even a cotton swab. You could do serious damage to your eardrums or canals. Ear wax, that sticky yellowish stuff inside, is something you're supposed to have. Wax acts like a magnet for dirt and keeps it from traveling into your ear canal. It's possible, though, to have too much wax. If your ears feel plugged, talk to your doctor to find out a safe way to get the gobs out.

Pierced Ears

If you want to get your ears pierced—and it's OK with your parents!—go to a professional who uses clean, sterile equipment. Allow two to three months for the holes to heal before you change earrings. Clean your newly pierced ears daily with a cotton swab dipped in rubbing alcohol. Redness, itching, or oozing near the hole might be a sign of infection. If this happens, call your doctor for advice.

Volume Control

It's OK to turn on the music and tune out the world, but don't turn up the volume! Over time, exposing your ears to loud noise can damage your hearing. Take this test: If someone next to you can hear sound coming out of your headphones or earbuds, the volume is too loud.

Many girls are allergic to the metals used in cheap earrings. To be safe, look for surgical steel, sterling silver, or 14-karat gold.

Swimmer's Ear

If you spend your summers at the beach or in the pool, you're a good candidate for swimmer's ear. This is an infection that occurs when bacteria in the water get into your ear and grow, causing a painful earache. The best way to prevent swimmer's ear is to dry out the ears and disinfect the insides. Follow these steps:

1. After you swim, dry your ears thoroughly with a towel.

2. Mix 1 teaspoon rubbing alcohol with 1 teaspoon white vinegar. Ask a parent or trusted adult to put a few drops in each ear. The alcohol helps dry out the ear, and the vinegar kills bacteria.

3. If you have ear pain, especially when you tug on your ear, see a doctor.

Eyes

It's a good idea to have your vision checked every year at school or your doctor's office. If you have trouble seeing things far away, such as a sign, you may be nearsighted. If you have trouble reading up close, you might be farsighted.

Be on the Lookout
Many girls don't notice problems with their eyesight until they have to do a lot of reading or looking at the board in school. This is often between third and fifth grades. You might need glasses if you have:
- headaches while or after you've been reading.
- trouble seeing objects at a distance or up close.
- double vision not caused by crossing your eyes.

Eye Exams
If you're having difficulty with your eyes, have them checked by an eye-care professional. Even if you aren't having problems, doctors say you should have an exam by the time you've begun to read. It's important to check for early signs of disease. At the exam, you'll be asked to read a special chart up close and at a distance. The doctor will look at your eyes through a kind of microscope and may put drops in your eyes to *dilate,* or enlarge, your pupils. This helps the doctor see inside your eyes, and it doesn't hurt at all.

"I just got glasses. I was worried everybody would make fun of me, but I realized that after a while, no one will remember what I look like without them!"

Courtney

You're in Good Company
Your vision may continue to change for a while until you reach your teens. If you're one of the first to get glasses, have fun picking out a pair you love and wear them with confidence. Within the next few years you might peek around and discover that many of your friends and classmates have joined the club!

Glasses

Glasses are convenient and easy to care for. They come in lots of cool colors and shapes. Think of your eyeglasses as fashion accessories—a great way to express your style!

Contact Lenses

Contact lenses change the way you see without changing the way you look. But they're also expensive and require daily care and cleaning. Some girls don't feel ready for this responsibility.

Eye Protection

Your eyes need protection from the sun, just like your skin does. Wear sunglasses at the pool or beach and on the ski slope to protect your eyes from ultraviolet rays. Look for shades marked "UVA/UVB protection." Don't stare into the sun, and never look directly at a solar eclipse, even with sunglasses.

Mouth

A bright smile can boost your mood and show the world your confidence. Make sure your smile is also a sign of good health by brushing up on the basics.

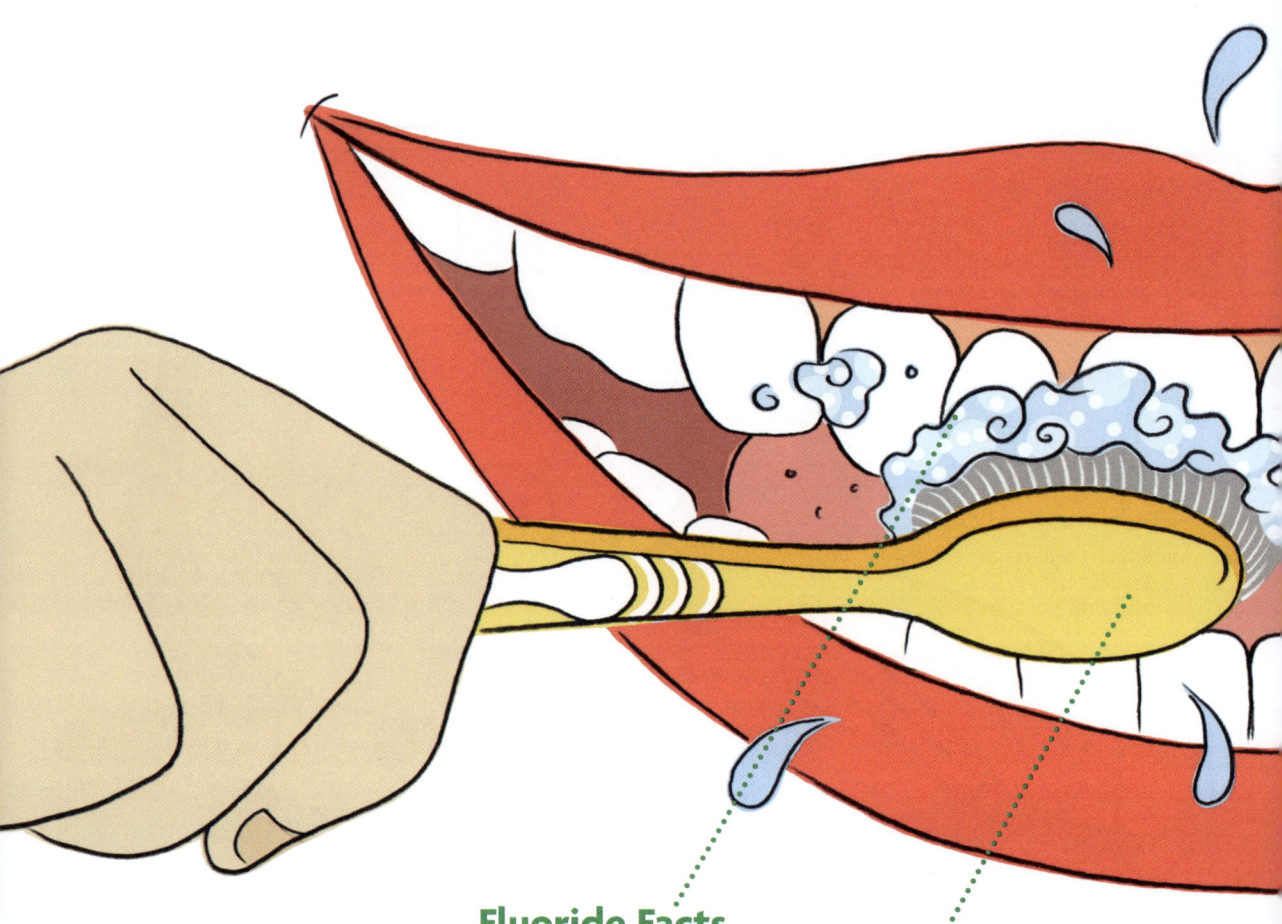

Fluoride Facts

Fluoride is a mineral that helps make teeth strong so they can resist cavities. If you live in a city, your water probably has some fluoride in it. Make sure your toothpaste does, too. And you don't need a huge gob of paste to get the job done—just a squirt about the size of a pea.

Toothbrush Basics

Whether you use a regular toothbrush or an electric toothbrush, look for a small brush with soft, rounded bristles. Replace your toothbrush—or swap out your brush head, if electric—every two to three months, or as soon as the bristles get droopy. Bent bristles won't clean your teeth properly, and they can harm your gums.

Attack Plaque!

Plaque is a gooey bacterial film that forms on your teeth. It can cause cavities and gum disease. Brush your teeth first thing in the morning and at bedtime. Try to brush after eating, too. Pack a toothbrush in your backpack and slumber party kit so you won't be tempted to skip. Do it every day, the right way. No fair just swishing the toothpaste around a little! Correct brushing takes minutes, not seconds. Many electric toothbrushes have built-in timers to make sure you brush long enough.

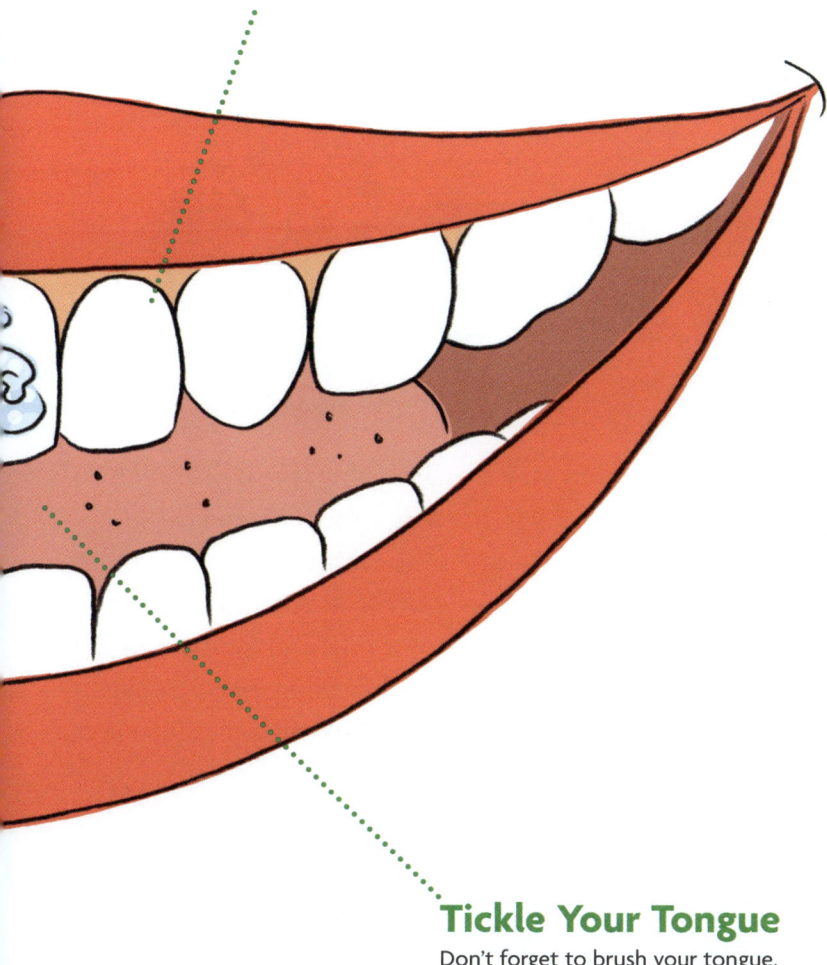

Tickle Your Tongue

Don't forget to brush your tongue, too! Freshly scrubbed taste buds are an important part of a clean mouth and fresh breath.

How to Brush

1. Hold your toothbrush at an angle to your gum line. Brush back and forth in small strokes, one tooth at a time. Repeat until you've scrubbed every single tooth.

2. Now do the back of each tooth, using the same back-and-forth motion. Make sure to brush right up to the gum line.

3. Use the tip of the brush to get behind your top and bottom front teeth.

How to Floss

1. Pull off a strand of floss about 18 inches long. Wind most of it around the middle finger of one hand, and the rest around the middle finger of the other.

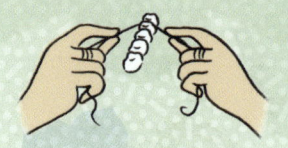

2. Grip the floss between your thumbs and forefingers, stretching it tight. Push the floss gently between two of your teeth, wiggling it up and down the sides of both teeth and under the gum line. Imagine yourself scooping out little bits of food.

3. Unwind a little clean floss, winding up the used floss as you go. Floss between two more teeth. Keep going, winding and flossing, until you've cleaned between all your teeth. Don't forget to floss at the very end of each row, behind your last tooth.

Healthy Gums

Think pink! Your gums need just as much attention as your teeth. If you don't take care of your gums, you could be setting yourself up for *gingivitis*—a disease that causes painful, red, swollen gums. To prevent gingivitis, floss once a day to fish out food lurking along the gum line. Dental floss comes in different thicknesses, waxed and unwaxed, to slide between your teeth comfortably. It even comes in tasty flavors!

Fresh Breath

Halitosis is a fancy way of saying "bad breath." But no matter what you call it, nothing shouts "Stand back!" quite as loudly. In rare cases mouth odor is caused by an infection, upset stomach, or other problem that may need a doctor's attention. But it might just be a sign that you're skimping on brushing and flossing. Food between your teeth can rot and stink just like garbage. Clean it out!

Smile and Say "Calcium"!

For strong chompers, eat foods high in *calcium*, a mineral that helps toughen up teeth. You can find calcium in dairy products such as milk, cheese, and yogurt, as well as in nondairy foods such as green leafy vegetables, black beans, and orange-colored fruits. A balanced, healthy diet that limits gooey, chewy, sticky snacks is the smartest choice.

Regular Visits

Does going to the dentist make your teeth chatter? You'll be less afraid if you know what to expect. Before the exam, ask your dentist to explain what will happen. And remember, regular checkups are the best way to avoid cavities and other problems that require special treatment.

Mouth Guards

If you play high-impact sports such as basketball or softball, you might want to use a mouth guard to reduce the risk of injury to your teeth and mouth. Your dentist can help you decide if you need one.

Braces

Braces are a short-term investment in your long-term smile!

Grin and Bare 'Em
Millions of Americans—kids, grown-ups, even movie stars—proudly sport tin grins. If you're about to get braces, you might be nervous or worried that braces will pinch or hurt. Information is your friend! Write down any questions you have so you're ready to meet with your orthodontist for the first time. An orthodontist is an expert on braces. She'll answer your questions, make sure your braces are comfortable, and give you tips and tricks for how to care for your braces.

"It hurt when I got braces, but my mom and I were prepared. We stocked up on soft foods like applesauce and oatmeal, and we made lots of smoothies!" — Ella

A special brush called an *interproximal brush* scoots into the tight spots. Ask your orthodontist how to get one.

Brushing
Brushing your teeth carefully is more important now than ever because food can get trapped on brackets and under wires. You should brush after every meal or snack. And at least once a day, devote several minutes to scouring all the nooks and crannies. If you don't, you may be in for a shock when your braces come off—an ugly line of tooth decay right where the braces used to be!

Flossing
With braces, it's especially important to floss your teeth daily. Most dentists say that bedtime is a good time, since you're more likely to slow down and do it right. Ask your orthodontist to show you how to thread the floss above your brackets. There's even a nifty tool that you can use.

No-Gos
Hard foods can break your braces, and sticky foods will get, well, stuck in them. Cut apples and carrots into bite-size bits, and say "later" to caramels and gummy candy. These sticky treats are worth giving up to have beautiful, straight teeth.

Rainbow Smile
Express your style every time you smile. You can choose bands for your brackets in all sorts of colors, from pastels to neon brights. Ask your orthodontist what choices are available to you.

Face

The skin on your face doesn't need a bunch of fancy lotions or potions—just a little tender loving care.

A Gentle Wash
Wash your face thoroughly at least once a day, especially at bedtime. Use a mild soap or facial cleanser—not a deodorant soap or a body bar meant to be used in the bath or shower. Use your hands or a soft, clean washcloth to gently wash your face. Use warm, not hot, water and rinse your skin well to remove all traces of soap.

Hands Off!
One of the best things you can do for your face is to keep your hands off it! Your fingers can spread oil and bacteria. When you do need to touch your face, use clean hands. And never pick at pimples—you could turn a tiny flare-up into a big-time breakout that leaves a scar.

Chapped Lips

If your lips are chapped, soothe them with a swoosh of lip balm. Look for one with sunscreen in it. Also, make sure you're drinking enough water. Dry, cracked lips may be your body's way of croaking "Help—I'm thirsty!"

The Skin You're In

The skin on your face is thinner and more sensitive than the skin on other parts of your body, so be choosy about what you put on it. Look for unscented soaps and products that are labeled *hypoallergenic*, which means free of ingredients that can be irritating. If your skin is oily or prone to pimples, choose facial products that are oil-free or *non-comedogenic*—not likely to clog your pores. If your skin is dry, dab moisturizer or lotion only on the spots where it's needed.

Acne

Almost everyone comes face-to-face with skin flare-ups at some time. But you don't need to lose your head over them.

Acne Attack

Zits! Blackheads! Whiteheads! All of these bumps and blemishes are part of the package known as *acne*. Acne can appear for several reasons. During puberty, your body produces more oil, which combines with bacteria and dead skin cells to clog your pores—and that causes pimples. Family history also makes some people more likely to get acne. If you feel like pimples are picking on you, you're not alone. Almost everyone will have a battle with skin blemishes at one time or another.

Striking Back

While occasional bouts of acne are practically unavoidable, you may be able to prevent a few blemishes from becoming a full-blown breakout.

Keep your face clean. Wash your face daily with a mild soap or cleanser, but don't overdo it. Harsh scrubbing and rubbing can irritate already bothered skin.

Don't pick at or pop pimples. The oils and dirt on your fingers will only fan the flames of a flare-up. Plus, you could cause a permanent scar on your skin.

Check out the drugstore. Acne products can provide some relief for mild breakouts. With a parent or trusted adult, cruise the skin-care aisle at the drugstore, and read the labels carefully. Products that contain benzoyl peroxide help reduce oil and get rid of dead skin. But steer clear of products that contain alcohol—they can dry out your skin.

Talk to your doctor. Severe, out-of-control acne may call for medical attention.

A product with benzoyl peroxide may irritate sensitive skin. Before putting it on your face, test a little on the inside of your wrist to see if it gives you a rash. If it does, don't use it!

Sun Sense

On bright, sunny days and on snowy days, too, always bring your "sun sense" along with you.

Here's an easy way to remember how to protect your skin from the sun:

Slip on clothing that covers your skin from the sun's rays.

Slap on a hat with a broad brim that shades your face, ears, and neck.

Slop on sunscreen before venturing outdoors.

No Safe Tans
Doctors agree: There's no such thing as a safe tan, and all types of skin can be damaged by the sun. Exposing unprotected skin can result in a blistering hot burn and eventually lead to skin cancer.

Protect Your Skin
The sun's rays are most intense between ten o'clock in the morning and three o'clock in the afternoon, but dangerous rays are present all day long. Remember, too, that the sun can damage your skin even on cloudy days and in winter. The sun reflects off the clouds and snow, making it extra intense.

Before you head out the door, be sure to slather on some sunscreen. Sunscreen products carry a rating called an SPF, or sun protection factor. An SPF rating of 30 means that the sunscreen protects your skin 30 times longer than if you had used nothing at all. Everyone should use sunscreen with an SPF of at least 30. Going swimming? Wear water-resistant sunscreen with an SPF of at least 45, no matter what color skin you have.

Reapply Often
If you're spending a lot of time outside, bring sunscreen along and reapply it every two hours. When you're at the beach or pool, it's especially important to put on more sunscreen after you get out of the water.

Beach Basics

Sandy beaches make the sun's rays even stronger. Take extra care by wearing lots of sunscreen and covering up with a hat and T-shirt. Of course, finding a shady spot to spend some time in is a good idea, too. Your skin will thank you!

Check Your Skin

If you find a growth or mole on your skin that you haven't noticed before, ask your parent or trusted caregiver about seeing a doctor for a skin check.

Body Talk

Do you feel as if the whole world can spot every spot on your face? Keep your chin up. And give people something else to notice—your confident grin!

Cold Sores

I have a big, ugly sore on my face right next to my mouth. My mom says it's a cold sore, but I don't even have a cold! This isn't the first time I've had this problem, either. How do I get rid of it?

Sore Spot

Cold sores, also called fever blisters, don't have anything to do with the common cold. They're caused by a virus similar to the one that causes chicken pox. While cold sores aren't serious, they can be an occasional nuisance. They often flare up when you're sick or stressed out, although there's no way to predict exactly when you'll get one. There are products you can buy at the drugstore to help get rid of the sores. If you have frequent, painful sores, your doctor might be able to prescribe stronger medication.

Freckle Face

I have freckles. I hate them and wish I could get some kind of lotion that would make my freckles go away. I need help!

Freckles

Freckles are a very common feature for people of all skin tones. They are harmless little pops of extra melanin—the pigment that creates the color of your skin. They can be light to dark brown or even rusty-red dots sprinkled across your face, arms, or shoulders. While there's not a thing wrong with having freckles, wearing a hat and sunscreen might prevent more from cropping up. You may feel that your freckles make you stick out, but flip the script and instead of hating your freckles, try to embrace them as a fabulous feature!

Bothersome Bangs

I just got bangs, but I've been having a problem with them. I've been getting pimples on my forehead. I've been washing my hair six times a week and putting medication on the pimples, but they still won't go away. Should I grow my bangs out?

Forehead Pimples

Not everybody needs to shampoo daily, but girls who are rocking bangs may find that keeping the hair there extra clean is helpful. Oils from your hair can irritate acne and make it worse. You'll also need to steer clear of hair products such as styling gels, sprays, and pomades that can leave a greasy film on your forehead. You don't have to banish bangs permanently, but you might need to pin them out of the way until your forehead clears up. Using headbands, barrettes, and other hair clips is a fun and fashionable way to keep your bangs out of the zit zone. Ask the person who cuts your hair for some tips.

Zapped by Zits

I am 10 years old, and I have 13 zits. I've tried everything to get rid of them, but they always come back. I don't even eat a lot of junk food. Recently people have been calling me pizza face. What should I do?

Pizza Face

It's hard to deal with people who make hurtful remarks about things that are a normal part of growing up, like acne. Your best bet is to ignore them, and not give them the attention they crave. In terms of your skin, the truth is that you probably can't zap your zits completely. Doctors agree that diet doesn't have much to do with acne, but your doctor might be able to recommend treatments that are right for you. Try to be patient and kind to yourself during these flare-ups. The good news is that most acne clears up in the late teen years.

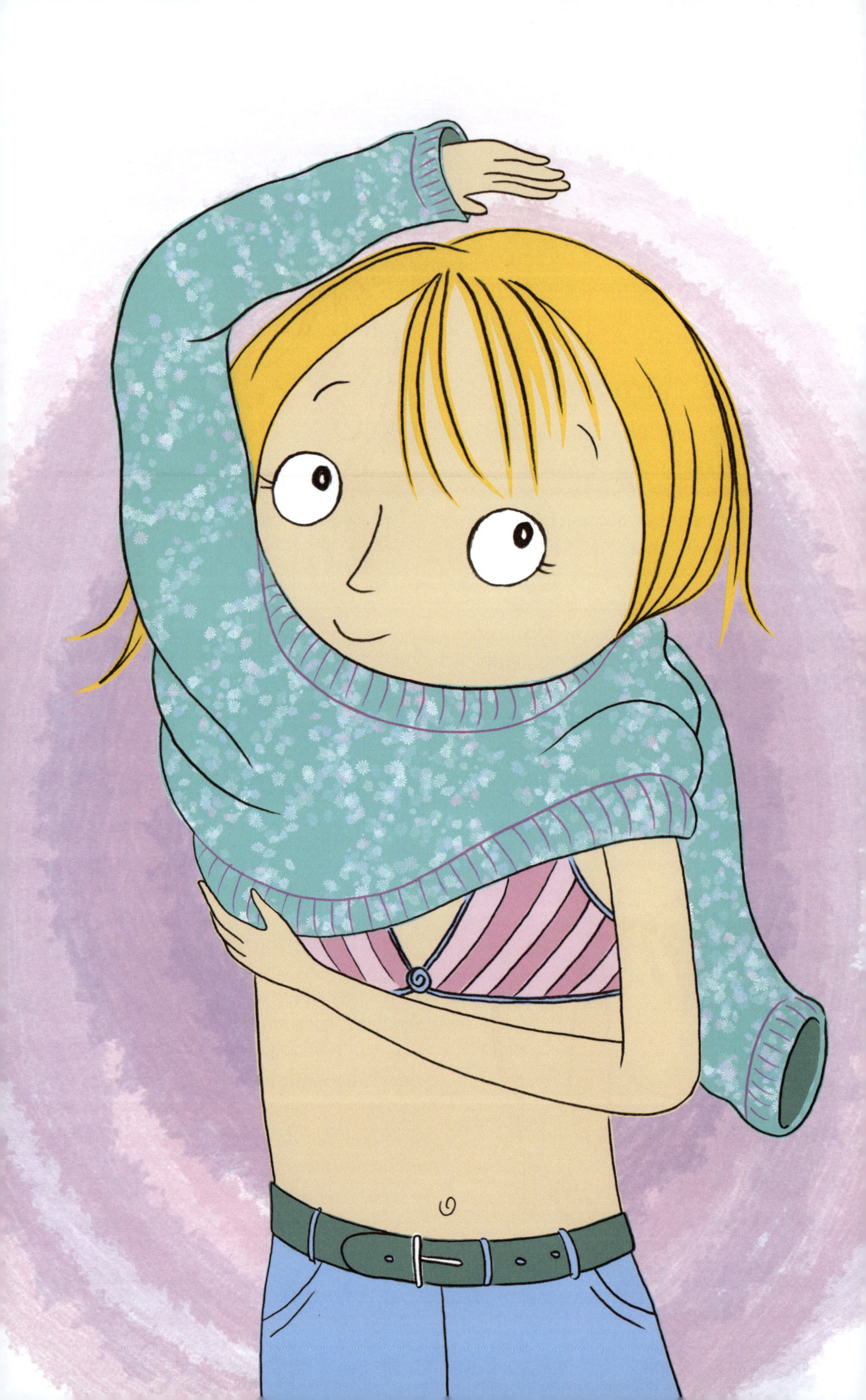

Reach

Here's handy advice for grooming your **hands** so they're as clean and healthy as can be. Plus everything you ever wanted to know about **underarms** and dealing with sweaty pits. And, finally, answers to all your questions about **breasts,** including hints for finding **bras** that really fit.

Hands

Give yourself a high five for solid hand hygiene! Keeping your hands and nails squeaky clean is one of the best ways to care for yourself and guard your good health.

Clean Hands Win!

Keeping your hands clean is your first line of defense against picking up germs and bacteria. While alcohol-based hand sanitizers are handy in a pinch, washing your hands with soap and water is always the best choice—especially before you eat and always after you use the bathroom. Scrub for at least 20 seconds. If you have a cold, wash up often—especially after you blow your nose!

Battling Bad Habits

If you bite your nails or suck your thumb or fingers, you're not alone. The good news is that lots of girls have been able to break their bad habits with one of these tried-and-true tricks:

- Hold on to a small object, such as a stone or a ball, to keep your hands busy and out of your mouth.
- Coat your nails with a special bad-tasting polish, available at the drugstore.
- Wear gloves or mittens to bed so you can't suck your thumb or fingers in your sleep.
- Set up a reward system. Use a calendar to keep track of how many days you go without giving in to your habit, and treat yourself when you meet your goal.

If all else fails, talk to a doctor or dentist for ideas. Don't give up—it takes time and patience to undo habits you've had for years.

Warts

Warts are harmless little bumps of flesh. They're caused by viruses passed from one person to another. Warts often go away by themselves but can take a long time—up to a year or two! To speed up the process, ask a parent or trusted adult for help using a wart-removing product (from a drugstore). Or try this: Put a piece of duct tape over the wart and leave it on for five or six days. Then remove it for a day to let the skin air out. Put a new piece of tape on for another five or six days. After a few weeks, your wart should be gone. If your warts are really annoying you, ask your doctor about removing them with a special freezing process.

Calluses

Calluses are hard, rough patches of skin caused by friction. Your body grows a layer of tough skin to protect the area. Athletes such as gymnasts get a lot of calluses, but you can get them just from raking leaves or gripping the handlebars of your bike. Wear gloves to help prevent calluses.

Nail Care

Scraggly, dirty fingernails are a germ hangout zone. Scrub your nails with a soft-bristled nailbrush to remove the dirt trapped underneath.

Once a week or so, use nail clippers to trim your nails. If you have a *hangnail*, a painful split in the skin alongside the nail, clip the hangnail down as closely as possible. Then leave it alone. Don't bite or pick at it. That will make it worse.

Use an emery board to round off any sharp corners or ragged edges.

Underarms

In the past you probably never gave your armpits a second thought. But now that you're growing up, it's time to start paying attention to them.

Antiperspirants help prevent pit stains. Your clothes will thank you!

BO—It's the Pits!
Sweating is natural and healthy. It's your body's way of cooling down. But you might be sweating more than ever before and in different places, such as under your arms. And when the sweat mixes with bacteria on your skin and meets the air, it can smell! Luckily, keeping body odor in check isn't hard. You can start by giving your armpits a good sudsing every time you shower or bathe.

Deodorants and Antiperspirants
Once you've washed your armpits, you may choose to use an underarm product that helps keep the sweat, odor, or both away. *Deodorants* work to prevent underarm odor. *Antiperspirants* work to reduce sweating. Some products are both an antiperspirant and a deodorant. They come in roll-ons, solid sticks, gels, and sprays—pick the one that works best for you. Some girls prefer to use underarm products that are made of natural ingredients and do not contain aluminum. It's also perfectly fine to just use soap and water to keep underarm bacteria in check, no special products needed.

Underarm Hair
If you haven't already sprouted hair under your arms, you will soon. Some girls don't like it. Others aren't bothered by it one little bit. Whether you want to remove it or leave it there is a very personal decision. If you feel you'd be more comfortable without underarm hair, ask a parent or trusted adult if you can remove it. Shaving is the most common way to get rid of underarm hair. While shaving might seem scary at first, it quickly becomes second nature. Ask a parent, trusted adult, or older sibling for a lesson.

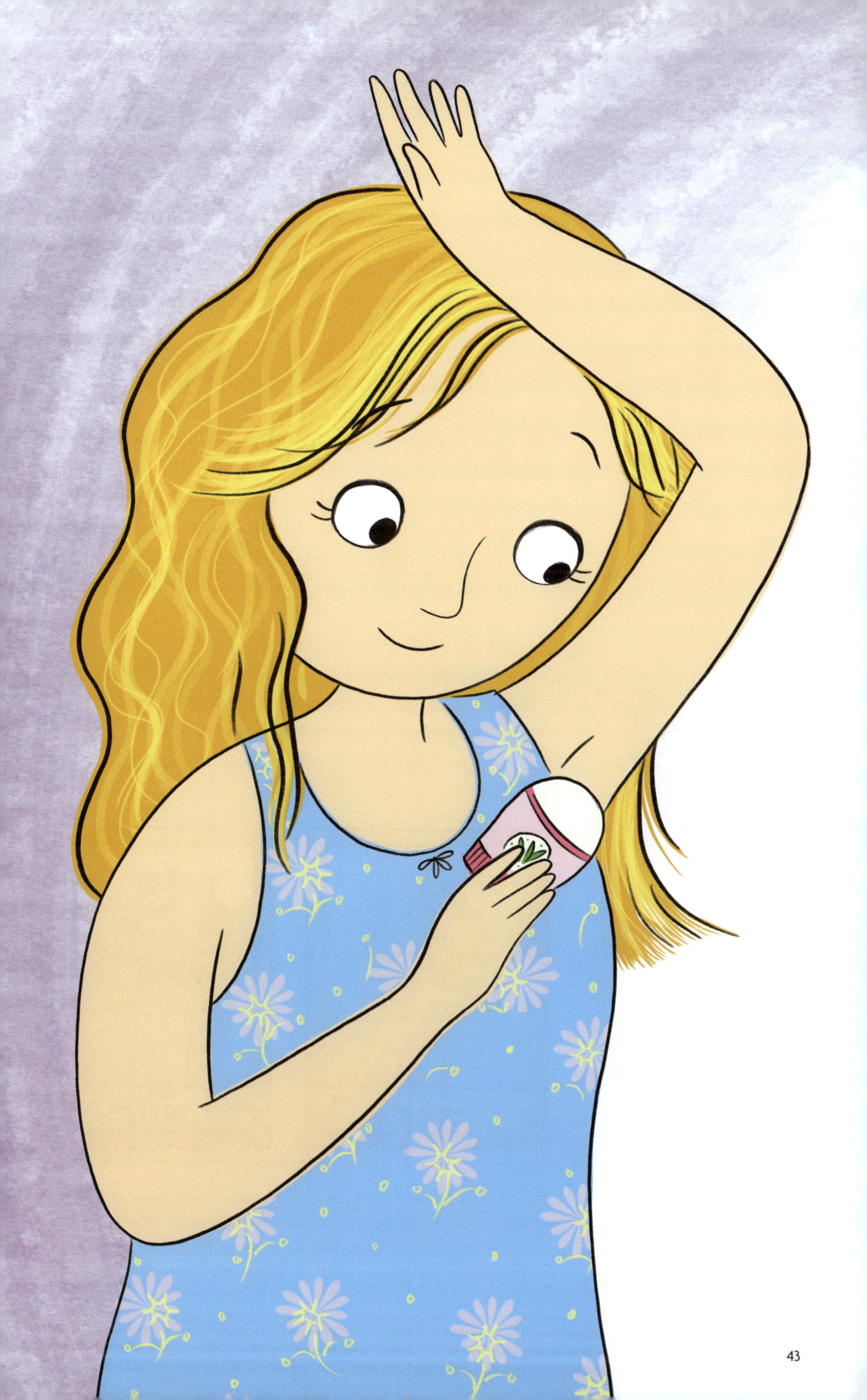

Breasts

Budding breasts are one of the first signs that you're entering puberty and that your body is starting to take on a new shape.

Time to Grow
You'll probably start to notice changes in your breasts between ages 8 and 12, although some girls start earlier or later. There's no way to predict how big your breasts will get—you won't necessarily take after your mother or older sister. And don't worry if you notice one breast growing more quickly than the other. They will eventually even out, although the two will never be exactly alike.

Stages of Development
Doctors divide breast development into the five stages shown below. See if you can tell what stage you're in, and sneak a peek at what's coming next.

If you don't seem to go through every stage, don't panic. Some girls skip over one of the middle stages.

Stage 1
This is how most breasts look before puberty begins. Breasts are flat to the chest, with a raised nipple and small areola.

Stage 2
A raised bump called a breast bud begins to develop under each nipple. The nipples and areolas get larger and darker. You might feel some tenderness in this area as the breasts grow.

How Long Does It Take?

There's no way to predict how long each stage will last or how long it will take for your breasts to become fully developed. Most girls reach stage 5 about four to five years after their breasts begin developing.

Shapes, Sizes, and Colors

Breasts come in endless varieties. Some are big, some are small. Some are round, some are more pointy. Some sit high on the chest, some hang low. Some point up, some point down. Even the colors of the nipples and *areolas*, the dark circular areas around the nipples, vary from pink to dark brown. Some nipples stick out, while others are *inverted*, or go inward. Some girls discover small hairs growing around their areolas. This is normal. Don't pick at or try to pluck out the hairs. Doing so can irritate the sensitive skin in this area and cause an infection.

Stage 3
The nipples and areolas continue to grow and can get even darker in color. Breasts get larger and may look a bit pointy.

Stage 4
The areola and nipple blend together into a mound that rises above the breast. Some girls skip this stage.

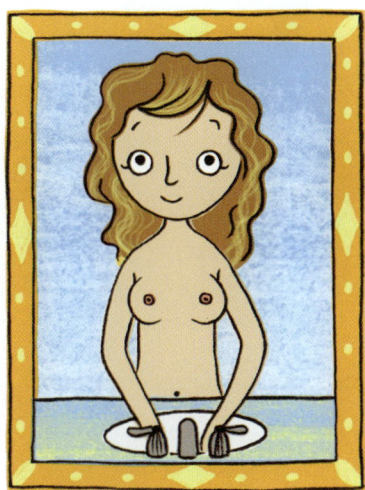

Stage 5
Breasts are fully developed, with a rounder, fuller shape. The areola and nipple form a mound that rises above the breast. The nipple is raised above it.

Bras

Do You Need a Bra?
There's no right answer to this question. There's only what's right for you. Do you feel self-conscious because your growing breasts show through your shirt? Are you uncomfortable when you play sports? Generally, you need a bra when you feel that you'd be more comfortable with one than without one.

"My friend started wearing a bra and wanted me to wear one too. But I wasn't ready. It has to be your own decision."

— Emma

First Things First
If you've decided it's time to get a bra, you'll need to talk with your parents or a trusted adult before you head to the store. Say that you feel you're ready for a bra, and ask if they will take you shopping for one. If they don't agree that you need one, offer to compromise by starting with a bralette (sometimes called a "training bra"). Bralettes are described on page 48.

No One Has to Know
What if you're ready to wear a bra but you're not ready for the whole world to know? Don't worry. Bras come in plenty of neutral colors that will match your skin tone. You don't have to buy the bras with bright colors or eye-popping prints that will show through your shirts.

Do you feel left out because everyone except you is getting a bra? Try a tank top or camisole under your shirt—no one will be able to tell if you're wearing a bra or not.

Sizing Up Sizes

Once you've decided to buy a bra, you'll need to figure out what size you wear. Bra sizes have two parts: a number and a letter. The number relates to the size of your rib cage. The letter—or cup size—relates to the size of your breasts. But don't worry too much about figuring out your exact bra size. It's only meant as a starting point. Every bra is different, and you might have to try on several different ones to find the right fit for you.

Adjusting the Fit

Once you've found the right size, you may still need to make some adjustments. Depending on the style of the bra, you might be able to tighten or loosen the fit around your rib cage by moving the hook over one or two notches. You may also be able to make the shoulder straps longer or shorter. To see if the straps are the right length, wiggle your shoulders. If the straps slide off, shorten them. If they feel as though they're digging into your skin, let them out a bit.

There's no reason to wear a bra while you sleep. It won't affect your shape or size. Put your bra on in the morning and take it off at night.

Find Your Size

1. Measure around your torso, just below your breasts to get your band size. Look on the chart to find the number for that size.

Torso size	Band number
24–25 inches	28
26–27 inches	30
28–29 inches	32
30–31 inches	34
32–33 inches	36

2. Measure around your breasts, over your nipples to get your chest size. Subtract the band number you got in step 1 from this size. Look on the chart to find your cup letter.

Chest size − band number	= Cup letter
−1	AAA
0	AA
1	A
2	B
3	C
4	D

3. Your bra size is your band number and cup letter. An example: 32A.

Bra Browsing

Bras come in oodles of styles, fabrics, and colors. You'll need to try on lots of them to find a good fit, so look for a store with a large selection. Ask your mom or a trusted adult to go with you. They can help adjust straps and fetch more sizes for you. When you find a bra that looks smooth under your shirt and doesn't pinch, scratch, or ride up your back, buy it!

Bralettes

A bra with thin straps and no built-in cups or padding is often called a bralette. This bra is lightweight and helps you get used to wearing a bra. Even if you don't need it for support, wearing one might make you feel less self-conscious and more confident about how you look.

Built-In Bras

Many tank tops come with a *built-in* or *shelf bra*. Because the bra is attached to the tank, most girls don't need to wear anything else supportive underneath. You might have noticed these bras in clothing well before you ever needed a bra—that's OK! There's no harm in having it in there.

Soft-Cup Bras

You guessed it—*soft-cup bras* are soft and flexible. For most girls who wear a size B cup or smaller, the elastic band in a soft-cup bra provides all the support they need, plus a comfortable fit.

Sports Bras

A *sports bra* looks like a cut-off tank top with a wide elastic band at the bottom. It's designed to hold your breasts snugly against your chest so that they don't bounce around while you're running or jumping. Sports bras aren't designed to be worn all day because they are tight and not super breathable, but they're great for sports!

Body Talk

Too big? Too small? No matter how they're built, many girls feel their breasts just aren't right. And that's just plain wrong!

Pump Up the Pasta?

I don't have any breasts! I was wondering if there were any foods to give me the nutrients to grow breasts.

Flat Chest

Lots of girls wish there were a miracle diet or magic exercise that would make their breasts blossom overnight. But no food you eat will make a beeline to your breasts. And all the push-ups in the world won't increase your cup size. Breasts are made mostly of fatty tissue and milk ducts, so there are no muscles in them to flex. Beware of advertisements for diets, drugs, or fancy gadgets that claim to boost your bust. Their claims are flat-out lies.

Body Bullies

Some of the boys in my class make fun of me because my chest is practically flat! They are always making up poems and songs about me.

Tired of Boys

Rude remarks can really sting! What you need to do is remember to look at the big picture. Are your breasts really the most important part of you? No way! What about learning to do a back flip, or your kindness to family and friends? That's the real you, the girl inside who really matters. Don't lose sight of her for a second, even when others seem to. If the teasing gets worse, or if someone's words or actions make you feel threatened or afraid, tell a parent, trusted adult, or teacher immediately. Nobody has the right to harass you or to make you feel unsafe.

Too Busty

I have bigger boobs than all of my friends. Because of this, my friends are embarrassed to be around me because they think I'm ugly and fat. I used to be popular, but now I feel dorky and lonely.

Desperate For Help

You're not dorky—you're developing. And though you wish otherwise, your body has a schedule all its own. It's wrong of your friends to tease or exclude you because of anything having to do with your body. Every body should be appreciated and respected. No one kind of body is best. Even though you feel hurt by your friends' behavior, stand strong and confident in the knowledge that your body is healthy and developing in a way that is completely normal. Soon your friends will be on their own paths to puberty. You'll have practical experience to share, and the wisdom to know that compassion and kindness are always the best way to lead.

Faking It

I am really flat-chested. All the girls have big breasts except me. Should I stuff? I'm worried the tissue might fall out when I'm running.

Stuff?

Who wants wads of itchy tissue stuffed in her shirt? You don't need that sort of trickery. Chances are you won't fool anyone, but you might feel like a fool when some eagle eye calls your bluff. Don't compare yourself to other girls or to people you see on TV or on social media. Every girl grows at a rate that's right for the way her body is built. Never forget that it's the stuff in your head and heart—not the stuff in your sweater—that makes you who you are.

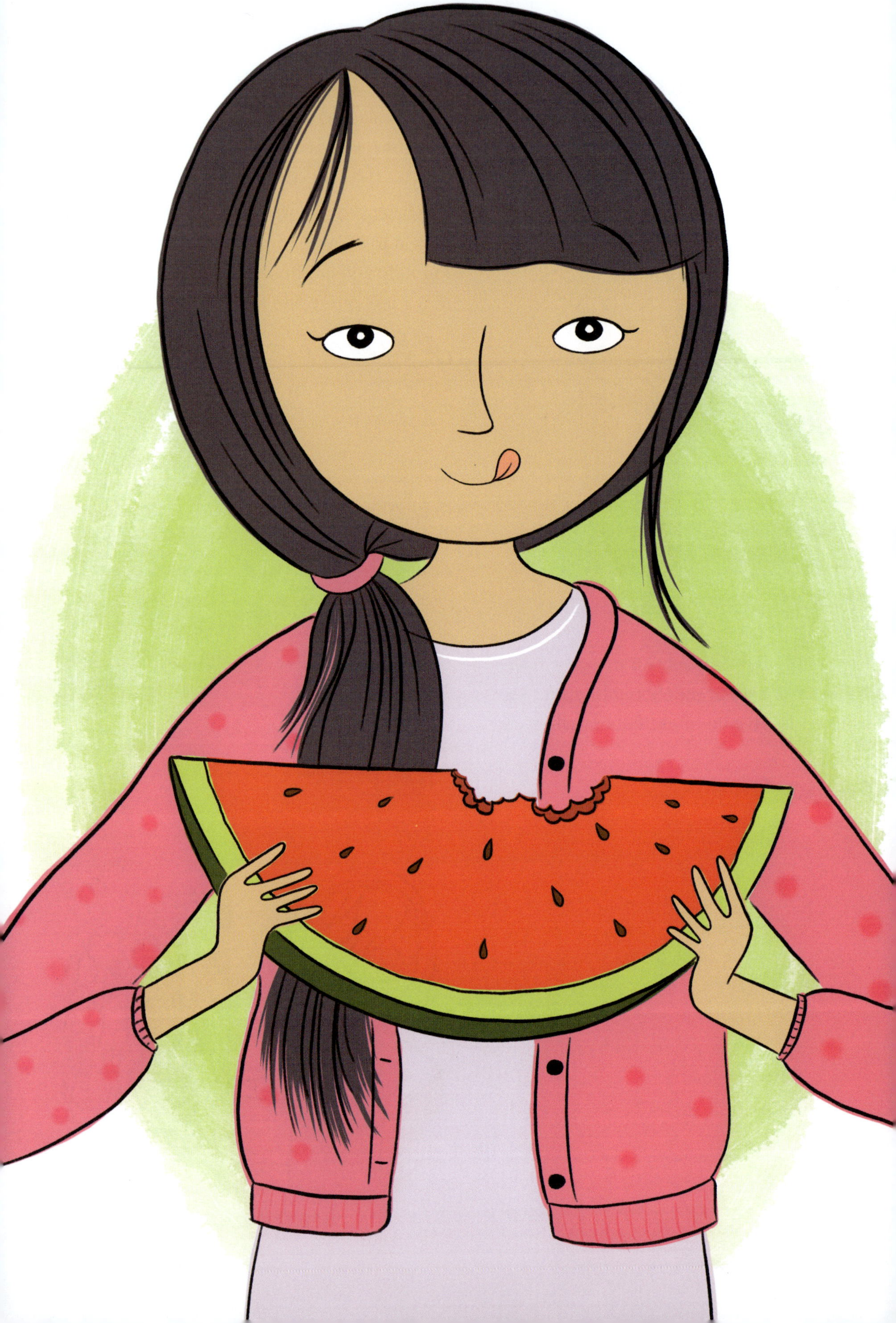

Belly Zone

This section is all about your midsection! Tall, short, straight, curvy—find out why all girls should celebrate their unique **shapes and sizes.** Learn how to listen to your body and nourish yourself with foods that will fuel you up and make you hum with good health.

Shapes & Sizes

All Different Shapes
The shape of your body—your basic frame—is something you're born with, like the shape of your nose or the color of your eyes. Some girls are tall and lanky, while others are short and sturdy. Some girls are curvy, while others are more straight. Usually your body shape resembles the shape of others in your family. No one body type is better or worse than another. All bodies are beautiful and deserve to be treated with love and care.

"Your weight depends on how your body is built. Also, your body hasn't finished developing yet. Just remember, you were made beautifully. Don't listen to anyone who says you're not!" —Sam

Beware of diets and fancy weight-loss programs you see advertised on social media or TV. Scientific studies show that they don't work for most people.

All Different Sizes
Many girls worry about whether their weight is "normal" for their age. But there's no such thing as one ideal weight, especially during puberty, when girls' bodies are growing quickly and changing shape. There's a wide range of weights that doctors consider normal for any girl, depending on her height and basic body type. Your doctor can help determine what range is right for you. One thing is certain: Your body will move through many ages and stages of development as you grow. You can learn to appreciate and celebrate your body exactly as it is now. This is a lesson that will serve you well through all the seasons of your life.

Where's My Waist?

As your body changes and your weight begins to shift, you might go through a period when your waist *thickens,* or gets bigger. Or your torso might grow to be straighter without a dip at the waist. Either development is completely normal and may change over time. No matter what shape you take, it's a custom fit that's unique and right for you.

Food

Fuel up! Eating delicious and nutritious food gives your body the energy it needs to grow during puberty.

Go for Balance
Eating the right way can seem confusing and overwhelming, even for grown-ups. There's a dizzying amount of information buzzing around—"Eat this!" "Don't eat that!" Here's the straight shot: A nourishing diet includes a balanced mix of vegetables, fruits, proteins, whole grains, and healthy fats. Each type of food has a special job to do. You need all of them to keep your body healthy and strong. There are no good foods or bad foods, only foods that are more or less helpful to feeling your best.

Listen for Cues
When to eat and how much to eat are different for every person. Your body sends you messages when it's hungry and thirsty. The trick is to tune in so you pick up on its cues. Eat when you're hungry. Stop when your body says it's full. When you have the time to do so, eat slowly and really savor your food, bite by bite. This makes your meals more satisfying and gives your body time to say, "Whoa, buddy, that's enough!"

Be Consistent
Try to have meals and snacks at about the same time every day whenever possible. Sticking to a schedule helps keep your energy level up and signals to your body that more fuel is on the way. It's best not to have a heavy meal right before bed. You'll catch more ZZZs and rest more comfortably if you have time to digest your dinner before you snooze.

Snack Smart

For many people, especially growing kids, three meals isn't enough food. Small snacks between meals can help power you through the day. Choose whole fruit like apples, bananas, and berries when you need an energy boost. Crunchy raw veggies are good on their own or with a tasty dip like hummus. Nuts and cheeses made from dairy or nondairy milks are smart choices, too. If you know you have a busy day, make sure you have a snack squirreled away in your backpack to hold you over until your next meal.

Treat Yourself Sometimes

Desserts are yummy and you should enjoy them when you have them, whether it's a slice of birthday cake, an ice cream cone, or s'mores around a campfire. The key is to balance treats with nutrient-rich foods, so that your body gets the fuel it needs every day.

Hydrate

Water is the best beverage around, and your body thirsts for it. Make sure you drink plenty of water every day, especially during and after exercise and when it's hot outside. Soda pop, fruit juices, and energy drinks are high in sugar and fake flavorings, so they shouldn't be your go-to's for quenching thirst.

Nutrition

Pack your meals and snacks with food that's nutritious and satisfying.

It's All in the Mix
Your food should be as delicious as it is nutritious! Go for lots of variety and keep it colorful. Whether your favorite foods are crunchy, spicy, chewy, or slurpy, try to "eat the rainbow" every day. Look for ingredients that are wholesome, fresh, and full of flavor so you'll glow inside and out.

Fruits, such as
- Berries
- Bananas
- Apples
- Pears
- Mangoes
- Peaches
- Oranges
- Melon

Vegetables, such as
- Kale, spinach, and lettuce
- Broccoli and cauliflower
- Carrots
- Celery
- Cucumbers
- Green peas
- Squash
- Tomatoes

Healthy fats, such as
- Nuts and seeds
- Olives and olive oil
- Avocados and avocado oil

Hit the Outer Aisles

The next time you go grocery shopping with your family, pay attention to how food is arranged in the store. Fresh fruit and vegetables, meat and fish, grains and nuts in bulk bins, dairy and nondairy milk, yogurt, and cheeses—a lot of the most nutritious stuff is found in the outer aisles. Head there first!

Be a Food Sleuth

Pay attention to how much added sugar is in many foods. Some sweeteners are easy to spot such as cane sugar, corn syrup, and fruit syrup. Others are hiding behind fancy names such as dextrose, fructose, glucose, and sucrose. Many packaged and processed foods have lots of salt (sodium) and fake flavorings, too. These ingredients may taste OK, but they don't give your body much nutrition to grow on, so try to keep them to a minimum.

Pick Nutritious Alternatives

Do you eat a vegetarian or vegan diet? Do you have food allergies or sensitivities to things like gluten, dairy, eggs, or nuts? No problem! There are lots of healthy choices available, from gluten-free pastas and breads to nondairy yogurt and cheeses. Be extra careful with packaged and processed foods. Eyeball labels to make sure they're free of ingredients you avoid. Look for options that are high in protein and enriched with calcium and vitamins so you get all the nutrients you need.

Proteins, such as
- Chicken and turkey
- Lean beef
- Salmon, tuna, and other fish
- Tofu, tempeh, edamame
- Milk, yogurt, and cheese
- Eggs
- Chickpeas and other beans
- Nuts and nut butters

What makes a person glow from head to toe? A daily diet rich in all the essential vitamins and minerals!

Vitamin A
For sparkling eyes, sharp night vision, and smooth skin, eat apricots, nectarines, carrots, spinach, sweet potatoes, and squash.

The B Vitamins
For healthy red blood cells and plenty of energy, eat meat, fish, poultry, whole-grain products, leafy green vegetables, and beans.

Vitamin C
For strong teeth, gums, and bones, and to ward off colds, eat oranges, strawberries, broccoli, peppers, spinach, and kiwi.

Vitamin D
For strong teeth and bones, drink vitamin D–fortified dairy or nondairy milk, and eat eggs, salmon, and liver.

Vitamin E
To protect the tissue in your skin, eyes, liver, and lungs, eat sunflower seeds, leafy green vegetables, nuts, and avocados.

Vitamin K

For blood that clots quickly when you're cut, eat kale, spinach, brussels sprouts, and other dark greens.

Iron

For a healthy blood supply that's full of oxygen, eat red meat, baked potatoes, apricots, raisins, beans, iron-fortified whole-grain breads, and dark leafy greens.

Calcium

For straight, tall posture and a great grin, eat yogurt, cheese, and broccoli. Drink three to four glasses of milk a day.

Body Talk

Weight worries and food fears can make some girls miserable at mealtime.

Am I Really OK?
I feel overweight. My doctor and parents say I'm fine but I don't feel comfortable in my own skin. Should I start dieting?

scared of weight

Bodies come in all shapes and sizes. But sometimes when girls see super-skinny people in ads and on TV, they get tricked into worrying about their own bodies. They see themselves as overweight when they're not. Do not go on a diet! Restricting food to lose weight is unhealthy for anyone. If you don't believe people when they say you're fine as you are, talk with with a parent, doctor, school counselor, or other trusted adult. They can help you see yourself clearly—and teach you to like what you see.

Friend vs. Others
My friend is always comparing herself to other girls. She's always saying that she's jealous of how thin and developed I am. It makes me sad that she thinks she's not good enough. But my friend isn't the only one who does this—lots of my friends do. Why?

Confused

Most girls compare themselves to other girls—especially during puberty, when everyone is changing at different times, in different ways. You might find yourself checking out everyone else to see where you fit in. That's normal. But here's the thing: When you compare yourself to others, it's easy to find things about your body that are different from someone else's. It might be hard, but girls have to learn to love how they're made and view themselves as equals. Next time your friend talks about being unhappy with her body, you can help her see herself in a kinder light. Say, "You're great the way you are. Let's not compare ourselves to other people; it's just not fair. OK?"

Junk-Food Junkie

I have a problem with eating junk food. I know junk food is not good for my skin, and sometimes it makes me feel tired and kind of yucky. How can I get off my urge to eat and eat and EAT junk food?
WORRIED

Eating junk food every now and then is not a health disaster. And doctors no longer believe that it causes skin woes. Junk food simply doesn't have much nutritional value—it fills you up without giving you the nutrients you need. It's not surprising that you feel low in energy if you eat it frequently. Aim to have most of your food be delicious, nutritious fuel for your body. Snacks like fresh fruit, cut-up veggies, or a handful of crunchy nuts can be super satisfying and quick to grab as you head out the door. Don't expect to cut junk food out of your life entirely. It's easier to allow yourself an occasional treat than to stick to a strict, junk-food-free diet.

Mirror, Mirror

I can't help it, I just hate the way I look. When I look in the mirror, a blob looks back at me. I'm miserable. I just feel too big, even though I know I'm not. What should I do?
Wondering

Even though your body is likely growing and changing exactly as it should be, it sounds as if your reflection is telling you a different story. Sometimes your brain can play tricks on your eyes. Many girls—and women, too—see themselves as bigger or smaller than they really are. It's important to see your body as it really is, so talk to a parent or another trusted adult about this. Their words might be just the reassurance you need to view yourself in a way that's true. If your worries continue, or if you find yourself tempted to alter the way you eat or exercise to change your appearance, you might need to consult a doctor to restore your sense of confidence and well-being.

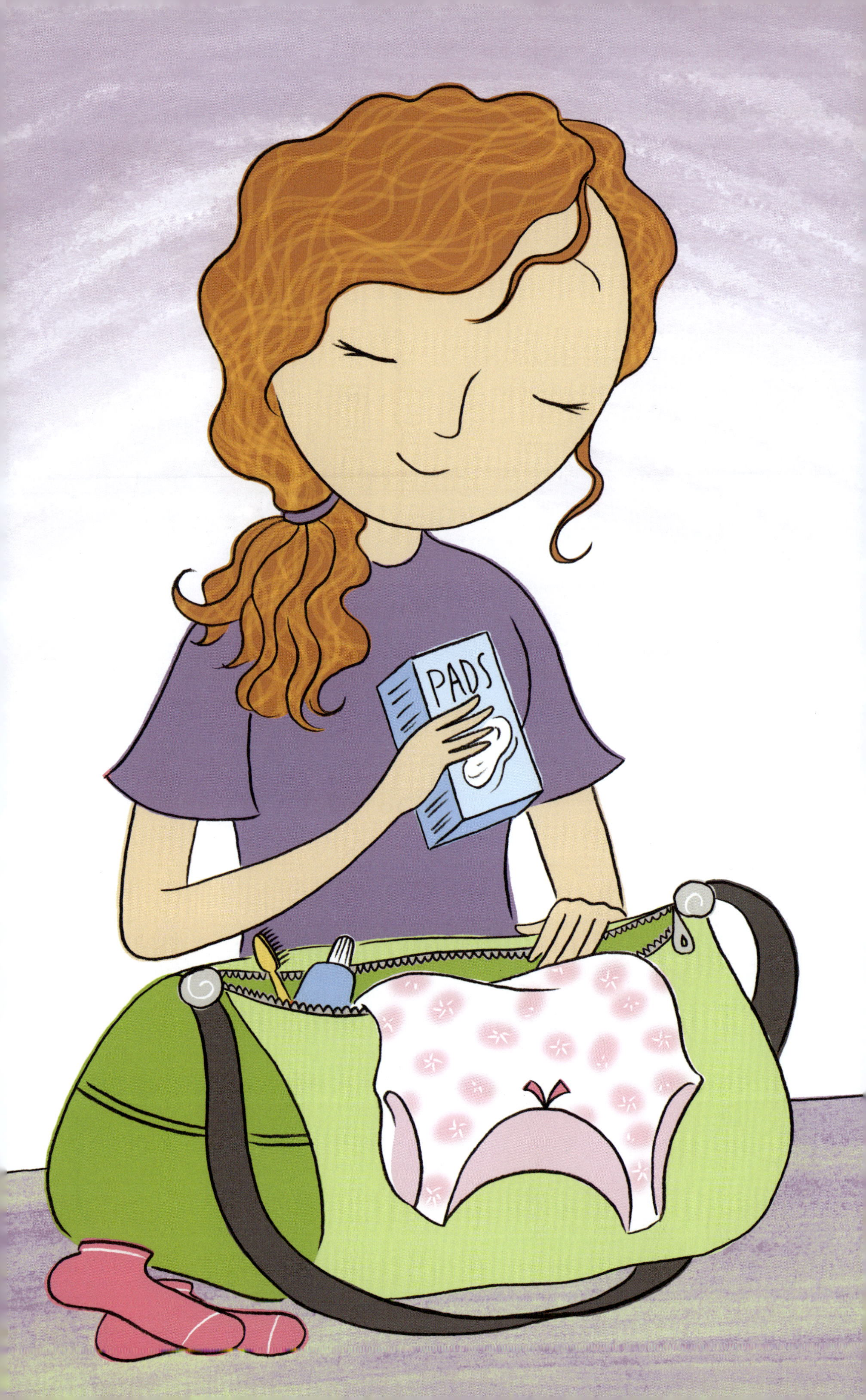
PADS

Big Changes

Whether you've already sprouted **new hair** and started your **period,** or whether you're still waiting for these big changes to happen, this section answers the important questions, from those about using **pads** to the ones seeking the truth about **PMS.** Armed with the facts, you'll be able to relax.

Pubic Area

The area below your belly button will undergo some pretty big changes during puberty.

Pubic Hair

As your body begins to change and develop, you will notice new hair in places that were once smooth. The pubic area is the triangular patch between your hip bones and thighs. Hair that grows here is called *pubic hair*. At first, the hair looks straight, kind of like the hair on your arms or legs. For many girls, it is dark—almost black—but for others it matches the color of the hair on their heads. Some girls have small patches of straight hair in their pubic areas from the time they are babies, and some notice it only when their bodies start to develop. For most girls, pubic hair takes a long time to appear. It eventually changes from fine, straight hair to coarse, curly hair.

Other Changes

You may notice a sticky liquid in your underpants. This is called *vaginal discharge*, and it is totally normal. It is coming from your vagina, is usually clear or whitish, and has very little smell. Your vagina makes the discharge to keep itself clean. Some days you might have none at all; other days you might notice it a couple of times.

If the discharge has a different color or a strong smell, this can be the sign of an infection. It can look greenish or white, and your vaginal area might even feel itchy or swollen. If any of these things is happening, talk to your parents or a trusted caregiver and see your doctor.

It's normal for pubic hair to appear over a period of years, so don't be surprised if this process seems as slow as watching grass grow.

Strip Clean
Take off damp or sweaty clothes as soon as possible. Bathing suits, tights, and leotards made of nylon and other synthetic fabrics can cause rashes and infections. Be sure to wash these garments frequently.

Get into Cotton
Whether you wear bikinis or briefs, buy underpants that are made of cotton or have a cotton lining. Cotton *breathes,* or lets moisture pass through and evaporate. That means less risk of irritation and infection.

Fresh Start
Put on a clean pair of underpants at the start of every day and after every shower or bath. It's the simplest way to stay fresh.

Period

Getting your period. Those three little words might make you feel curious, excited, and nervous all at the same time.

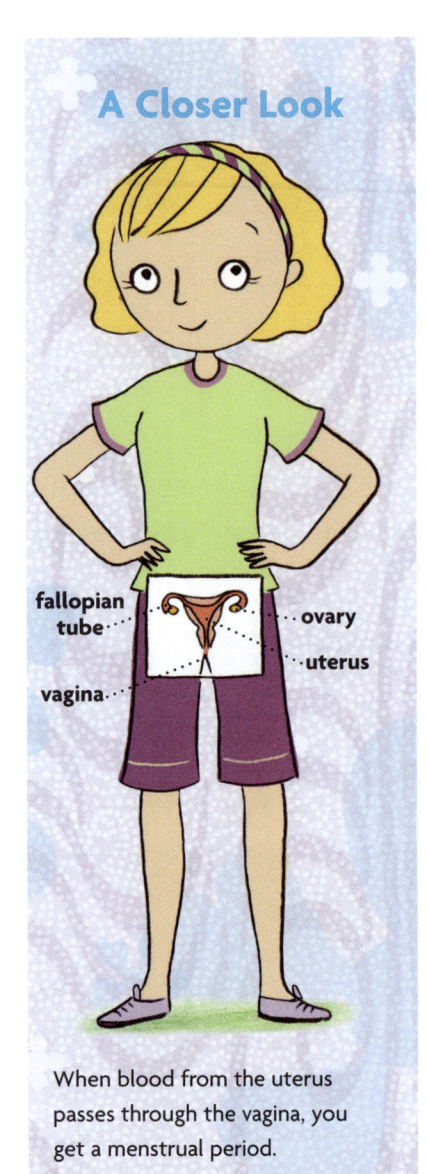

A Closer Look

fallopian tube
ovary
uterus
vagina

When blood from the uterus passes through the vagina, you get a menstrual period.

The Basic Facts

So, what's a period, anyway? It's short for *menstrual period*—the time each month when fluid containing blood flows out of the *uterus* through the vagina. The amount is small, about 3 tablespoons. This flow usually lasts two to eight days. Some girls have a menstrual period every 25 days. Other girls get them up to 40 days apart. All are normal. When you first start getting your period, though, the length of time between periods—and the number of days the flow lasts—may change each month. After a while, your periods will become more regular.

Periods are a sign that your body is healthy and working properly. It's preparing to do the grown-up work of having a baby someday. Every month your body practices for this by building a "nest," a place for a baby to grow inside your uterus. The nest is a lining of blood and other fluid that forms inside the uterus. Because there's no baby, the lining is shed and you have a period. It's all controlled by *hormones,* the chemicals that change your body from little girl to grown-up woman.

Telltale Signs

Most girls start to get periods between ages 9 and 15. You can't predict exactly when you'll get your first period, but your body might give you clues that it's on its way. Most girls start to *menstruate,* or get periods, a couple of years after their breasts have started developing and their pubic hair has begun growing in. Can other people tell whether you've gotten your period yet? Nope! Not unless you tell them.

Your First Time

So the day comes when you get your period. It might announce itself with a bright red, rusty red, or dark brown stain in your underpants. What do you do? Don't panic. Wipe yourself as well as you can. If you don't have a pad or tampon—or you don't know how to use one—fold up some toilet paper, tissues, or paper towels to put into your underwear.

Find a parent, an older sister, or an adult you trust. Take a deep breath and say, "I think I just got my period. Do you have something I can use?" You may feel a little awkward, but remember, getting your period is normal. There's no reason to be ashamed. The older person will probably remember how it felt her first time and will be glad to help.

Keep a supply of pads or tampons on hand so you're always prepared. You might even keep a little pouch of supplies in your backpack or school locker. Once you know you won't be taken by surprise, you can R-E-L-A-X.

If your period catches you by surprise at school, ask a teacher or school nurse for help.

Buying Supplies

Deciding which period care products to use might seem overwhelming at first. You can choose pads, period underwear, or tampons. The trick is to find which products work best for you. Your preferences may change over time, too, once your periods become more regular. You can even pick different products depending on whether you will be at home or out and about for the day. When girls first get their periods, most start with pads or period panties. Many girls don't try tampons until they're older. You can talk to your mom, older sister, or another trusted adult to figure out where to start.

Pads

Pads are convenient and easy to use. Almost all pads have a sticky strip on the back that attaches to your underpants. Others have wide "wings" that wrap around the edges of your underpants for added coverage.

Panty Liners

Panty liners, or panty shields, are very thin pads. They're best for days when your flow is light, or when you suspect your period might start and you want to be prepared. Some girls like to wear a panty liner or period underwear along with a tampon in case the tampon leaks.

Tampons

Tampons are good for sports, especially swimming, because they're worn inside the body. The vagina muscles hold the tampon in place so it can't slip out. A string hangs outside your body so you can pull the tampon out.

Scented or Unscented

Most pads and tampons are available in both scented and unscented versions. Scented products have perfumes and other chemicals to fight odor caused by fluids and moisture trapped in the pad or tampon. But they can also irritate skin and cause allergic reactions. You're better off using unscented products and keeping yourself fresh by changing your pads and tampons regularly.

Period Underwear

Period panties look and feel like regular panties but are sewn with several layers of absorbent, leak-proof fabric in the crotch. Instead of throwing them away like a pad or tampon, you simply rinse them in the sink and wash them with the rest of your laundry. They're thrifty, comfy, and eco-friendly.

When to Change

It's a good idea to replace your pad or tampon every two to four hours to prevent leaks and odor. If you have to go to the bathroom in the meantime, you can hold the string of the tampon out of the way so it doesn't get wet. Never leave a tampon in place for more than six to eight hours. At night, use a pad or period underwear, which can be worn for many hours depending on which ones you choose. Change pads and period underwear right before you go to bed and again first thing in the morning.

What to Do with the Used Pad or Tampon

Whether you're at home or away, be sure to dispose of your used pads, tampons, applicators, and outer wrappings appropriately. This means wrapping pads in toilet paper and placing them in a wastebasket. Some public restrooms have a bin in each stall for this purpose. Never flush a pad or tampon down the toilet. Some tampon applicators are flushable. Check to see if the box says "flushable applicators." If not, wrap the applicator in toilet paper and throw it out.

Wrappers from tampons and pads go in the wastebasket—not in the toilet.

Caring for Period Underwear

Because period panties are reusable, they require a little extra care. After wearing, rinse them in cold water to remove as much blood as possible. Then you can throw them in the washing machine with your other laundry, but don't put them in the dryer—these panties should air dry. Check your underwear's care instructions for more details. If you will be swapping out period underwear during the day, you might want to keep a spare pair and a plastic bag for the worn pair in your backpack or tote.

Is It Over Yet?

Once your periods become regular, which can happen right away or in a few years, they should last about the same length of time each month. You'll be able to tell when your period is winding down because the flow is usually heaviest in the beginning or middle and then starts to trickle off toward the end. You might not notice any blood for several hours or even a whole day. The color may change, too—from bright red to brown. It's a good idea to wear a panty liner or period underwear for a day or two even after you think your period is over. If you go more than two days without seeing any blood, your period is probably finished.

Keeping Track

At first, it can be tricky to predict when your periods will arrive. Use a calendar to keep track of when they start and end. After a while, your cycle should become regular enough for you to be able to figure out when to expect your period.

Tampons

Most girls use pads when they first get their period. But eventually, some girls switch over to tampons. There is no rush to do this—it's a very personal choice and one that you will want to discuss with your mom or other trusted adult or caregiver.

When girls first start using tampons, they generally pick the smallest ones. These are called "junior," "slim," or "slender." These tampons are skinnier and smaller than other types, so they are easier for girls to use.

Most tampons come with an *applicator*, which is a pair of tubes that help to insert the tampon. Some girls find that plastic applicators (compared to cardboard applicators) are easier to use at first. The applicator does not stay inside your body. Once the tampon has been inserted, the applicator comes out and should be thrown away in the trash. There is more information about tampons in *The Care & Keeping of You 2* and in the instructions provided inside tampon boxes.

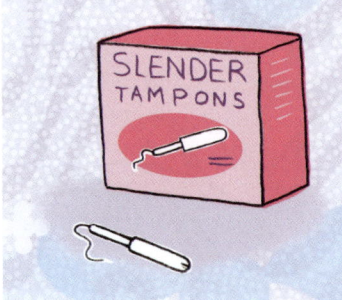

How to Use a Pad

Pads are a great choice when you first get your period. But while they're simple to use, they do take some getting used to. Follow the steps below to help you through your first time.

1. Get Ready

You can put a pad in your underpants anytime you want. Some girls like to wear thin pads every day because of vaginal discharge, and that's fine. When you have your period, though, you'll probably want to use thicker pads because they absorb more fluid.

2. Unpeel

If the pad comes individually wrapped, remove the packaging. Remove the paper covering the tape on the back of the pad, and lay the pad inside your underpants so that it fits along the crotch. If the pad has wings, fold those around the edges of your underpants after you have placed the pad.

3. Check the Fit

When you pull up your underpants, the pad might feel a little bulky—that's OK. It shouldn't irritate your thighs or prevent your underpants from being pulled all the way up. Make sure the pad sits in the middle of the crotch of your underpants—not too far forward or too far back.

4. Remove It

Most girls change pads each time they go to the bathroom. If your flow is heavy, you might want to change pads more frequently. Remove the pad by peeling it off your underpants from one end; then roll the pad onto itself from one end to the other. You can wrap the rolled pad in a piece of tissue or toilet paper and throw it away in the trash. Wash your hands.

Pad Pointers

There are so many different shapes and sizes of pads available. How do you know which ones to use?

Panty liners are super-thin pads. Most girls use them at the very end of their period when there is only a little bit of bleeding. Some girls even use them when they don't have their period because they don't like the feeling of vaginal discharge.

Regular pads are thin but they are very absorbent. These pads are usually longer than panty liners and hold more blood. They can be used anytime during your period, though if your flow is heavy, you will need to change your pad more often.

Maxi pads are almost as thin as regular pads, but they are much more absorbent. Maxi pads are great for heavy flow days.

Pads with wings are pads (panty liner, regular, or maxi) that have extra material on the sides. This material helps absorb blood that might leak over the edge of a pad. This helps keep your underpants nice and clean. When you use a pad with wings, tape the main part of the pad down first and the wings second. When you remove the pad, lift up the wings first and the main part second.

What Is PMS?

Once you begin to menstruate regularly, you may notice some patterns in how you feel right before your period. Sometimes these physical and emotional changes are referred to as *premenstrual syndrome,* or PMS for short. It's not a disease or an illness, just a natural part of your menstrual cycle. PMS is caused by hormones—natural chemicals that are in charge of the menstrual cycle. The symptoms you feel can be a clue to when your period is coming, so you'll want to pay attention to them.

Physical Signs

A week or two before your period, your breasts may feel swollen or more tender than usual. You might also notice that your body feels heavier, even puffy, and that your skin is more prone to breakouts. All of these symptoms will go away after your period begins. You may also feel cramps in your lower abdomen or back before and during your period. The cramps happen because the muscles of the uterus are hard at work.

Emotional Signs

Your period can also affect your mood. Some girls feel tired, irritated, grouchy—more emotional—in the days leading up to their period. If you find that your feelings are more intense during this time, know that this is perfectly normal. But when you're feeling extra edgy, try not to unleash your frustration on family and friends. Instead, try talking about how you feel. Doing so may bring kind words of support just when you need them most. And don't forget to treat yourself to some quiet time alone. Listen to music, take a walk, or write in a journal. You'll be glad you did!

Your feelings are important, so pay attention to them. Don't let anyone tell you they're stupid or silly or that they don't matter.

How to Feel Better

The best remedies for premenstrual aches and pains are fairly simple: eat wholesome, nutritious meals; exercise; give yourself a break when needed; and treat yourself to some soothing heat.

Ahhh—Heat!
A warm bath or a hot-water bottle laid over your tummy can help soothe cramps.

Aches and Pains
If you're struggling with headaches, backaches, or cramps, talk to a parent, trusted adult, or your doctor about what's right for you.

Skip the Salt
Cut down on salty foods such as pretzels and chips before your period. Salt makes your body retain water, giving you that puffy, bloated feeling. Eat plenty of fruits and veggies instead.

Exercise
Stay active! Exercise is a great way to ease aches and pains and to lift your spirits, too. A brisk walk, a few laps in the pool, some gentle yoga, or a bike ride in the fresh air is always good medicine.

Body Talk

If you feel like your menstrual cycle is taking you for a ride, don't worry. In no time at all, you'll learn to take your periods in stride.

Sneak Attacks

What if my period starts in school or in church or in a public place and I don't have a pad or tampon? And what if it leaks on my clothes before I can stop it?
Scared

If you get caught unprepared, don't panic. Make a temporary pad out of folded toilet paper, facial tissue, or paper towel to put in your underpants. Then ask the school nurse, a teacher, or a friend if she has a spare pad or tampon. Some public restrooms have machines that dispense pads and tampons. If you do leak, tie a sweater, shirt, or jacket around your waist to make a fashionable cover-up until you can change clothes. Chances are, nobody will notice a thing! P.S. Cold water is best for getting blood stains out of clothes.

Pads, Tampons, Period Undies?

How am I supposed to know if a tampon, pad, or period underwear is right for me?
Just wondering

It all depends on what you're most comfortable with. All are safe and reliable if used properly, so you really can't go wrong. Some girls who play sports prefer tampons because they don't show through a uniform or bathing suit, and they can be worn in water. Some girls like tampons because they keep you feeling dry—you can hardly tell you have your period! Some girls don't feel ready for tampons, and like the comfort of period underwear—you can even get period swimsuits that are leak-proof. But other girls like pads because they're so simple to use. They're easy to change, and easy to know when to change. Don't be afraid to experiment to figure out which you like best.

Miserable, Period.

I've had my period for a year now, and I still haven't gotten used to walking around feeling like I've wet my pants. I'm the only one of my girlfriends who has it. My mom is here to talk to me about it, but I don't want to. I don't want to keep it to myself, either. I feel like I don't even want to grow up!

I don't want to grow up!

You sound lonely, scared, and uncomfortable, and that's a heavy load for any girl to bear. For starters, it might help to change your pad more often or consider giving period panties or tampons a try. Both will make you feel drier. Next, you need to find your courage—every ounce you can muster—and talk to an adult you trust. If you can't face your mom, pick an aunt, a teacher, a doctor, or a school counselor. It might be hard to imagine now, but talking it out with an adult who has "been there, done that" will make you feel much better.

Left Out

Everybody in my class has become a "woman" and I am still just a "girl." When everyone talks about being "women," I just hang back.

Maxi Pad

It's heartbreaking to feel that your friends are leaving you behind just because their bodies are changing at a different pace than yours. But that doesn't make these girls "women." There's a lot more to being an adult than getting your period and growing breasts. Still, your classmates may be feeling excited about the changes they're going through, maybe even a little afraid. And that's why they need to talk about them so much. Instead of feeling left out, can you listen in? Ask your friends questions about their experiences. You may get firsthand information that will help you when your day comes.

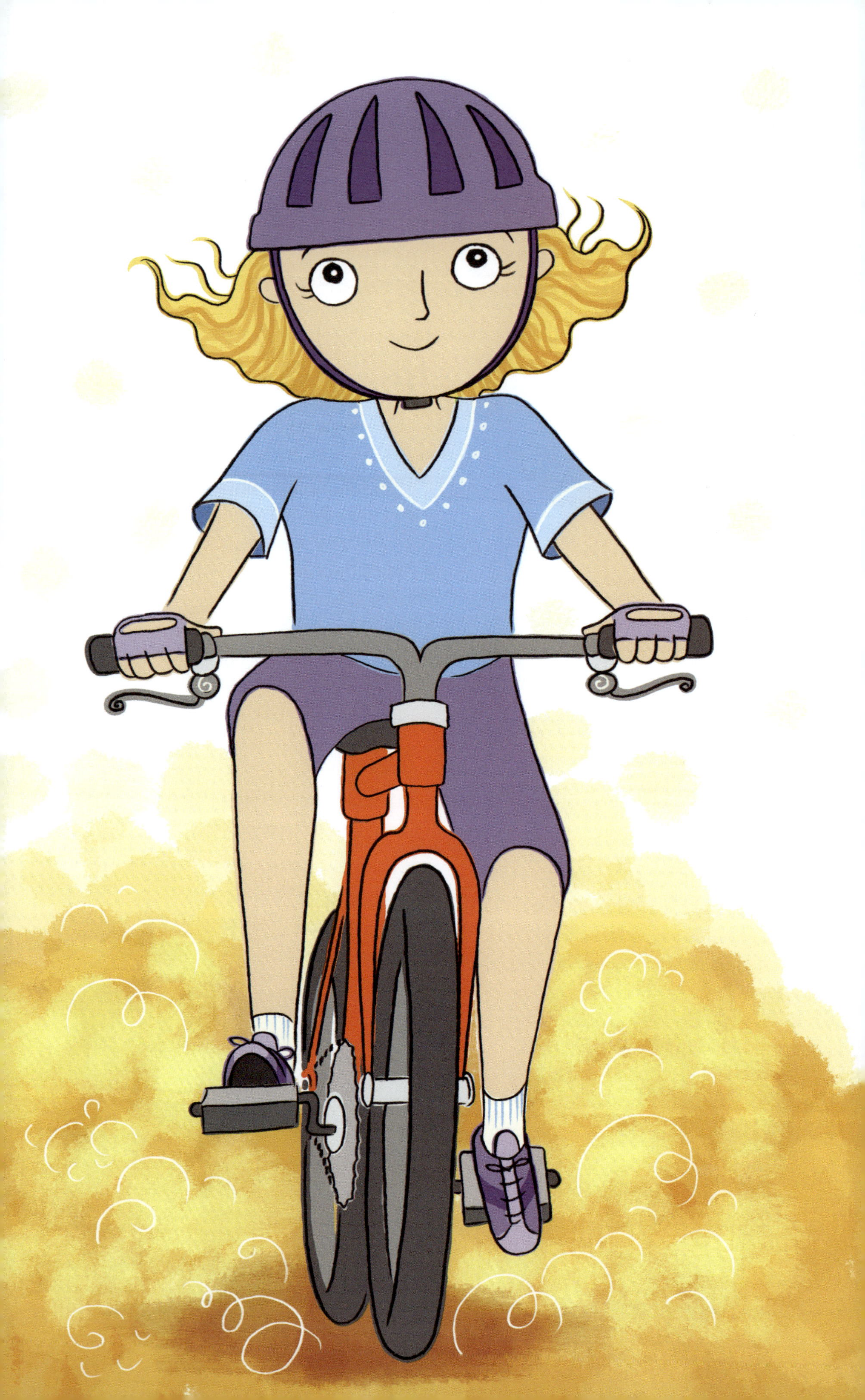

On the Go

Get a leg up on your growing **legs** and protecting your **feet** from pain and odor. Learn how to turn **fitness** into fun, and to practice **sports safety** with the right equipment, exercises, and first-aid basics. And when it's time to **rest,** here's advice on how to get a good night's **sleep** so you can start every day fresh and ready to get into gear!

Legs

Give your legs a hand for all that hard work they do to keep you up and running!

If you think you're ready to start shaving your legs, talk it over with a parent or trusted caregiver first.

Growing Pains
During puberty, you're going to shoot up in height. Your legs in particular are going to lengthen and grow. For a while, you might feel as if your body is all legs. This rapid growth may also cause a tired, achy, cramped feeling in your legs. These occasional *growing pains* usually go away after puberty. And don't worry if your legs seem out of proportion for a while—the rest of you will soon catch up!

And Growing Hair
About the time you start to grow hair under your arms, you may notice that you're sprouting more hair on your legs, too. Though there's no reason to remove leg hair, some girls prefer the look and feel of smooth shins. Whether to shave or not is a personal choice based on what's right for you. It's fine to experiment. See whether letting your hair grow naturally or removing it feels better. You might even want to switch back and forth with the seasons.

Shave Where?
Some girls shave only the hair on their shins and calves, south of the knees. The hair above the knees might be so fine that it's not worth the bother to remove it.

How to Shave

1. You'll need the help of a trusted adult to buy a razor. Disposable razors are easy to use but good for only a few shaves. A razor with replaceable blades is less wasteful, but changing the blades can be tricky.

2. Get your legs good and wet. You're more likely to nick yourself if your skin and hair aren't thoroughly moistened. Lather on a generous amount of soap or shaving cream or gel.

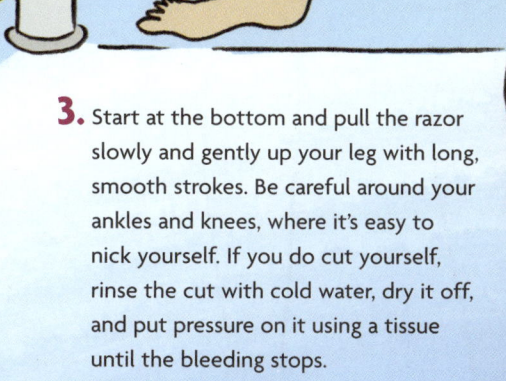

3. Start at the bottom and pull the razor slowly and gently up your leg with long, smooth strokes. Be careful around your ankles and knees, where it's easy to nick yourself. If you do cut yourself, rinse the cut with cold water, dry it off, and put pressure on it using a tissue until the bleeding stops.

4. Stop to rinse your razor often so it doesn't get clogged with hair. When you're done shaving, rinse the razor before storing it away. As a courtesy to other family members, rinse out the shower or tub, too.

5. After drying off, apply some lotion to your legs to soothe and moisturize the skin.

Feet

Your feet take a lot of pounding! Don't let foot and toe woes leave you standing on the sidelines.

P.U.! Foot Odor

The best way to deal with foot odor is to prevent it. Don't go sockless when you wear close-toed shoes. Wear clean cotton socks that absorb sweat, with shoes made of natural materials such as leather or canvas that let feet breathe. Fleece boots and footwear made from plastic and other synthetic materials are a recipe for smelly, sweaty feet. To de-stink your shoes, sprinkle baking soda in them and let them sit overnight. Shake out the baking soda—and the smell—in the morning.

Ouch! Blisters

Blisters are sore spots that develop where your shoes rub against your skin. The friction causes the skin to form a bubble, which sometimes pops or tears open. Don't pop the blister yourself. Place a bandage over it to protect it until the skin can heal. You may want to remove the bandage at night to expose the blister to air. This helps speed the healing.

On Your Toes

To keep your toes in tip-top condition, give them a little extra attention.

- When you shower or bathe, be sure to scrub between your toes. Use a nailbrush to scour under the nails.

- Trim your toenails regularly after showering or bathing, when the nails are softest and easiest to cut. Use nail clippers to cut straight across. This helps prevent *ingrown toenails,* which occur when a sharp corner of the nail grows into the skin.

- Give your toes room to wiggle! Never buy shoes that don't fit, no matter how much you like them—you'll be in too much pain to enjoy how you look.

Itchy! Fungus

You don't have to be an athlete to get *athlete's foot,* a fungus that spreads in damp places where people go barefoot, such as locker rooms and pools. You can prevent it by wearing flip-flops or shower shoes. If you notice itching and peeling between your toes, you may have a case. It's easy to treat with powders and sprays from the drugstore, with help from a parent or trusted adult. Air also helps athlete's foot go away. At the end of the day, take off your shoes and socks and wash and dry your feet. Then let them air out!

Fitness

Whether it's skateboarding or swimming, kickball or karate, find a fun way to move your body and elevate your heart rate. You'll boost your energy and mood at the same time!

Whatever your level of fitness or physical ability, you can find activities that are a good fit for you. Try out a few until you find what you love to do.

Active Girl = Healthy Girl

You already know that eating a nutrient-rich diet is essential to growing up strong. But regular exercise is just as important. In addition to helping you feel fantastic, exercise strengthens your heart, gives you energy, helps you sleep better, makes your muscles stronger and more flexible, and builds self-confidence. So get up, get out, and get into gear!

How Much Is Enough?

Doctors and fitness experts recommend at least one hour of physical activity every day, with most of this being aerobic exercise. *Aerobic exercise* is any activity that gets your muscles working with rhythm (like running, jumping rope, biking, dancing) so that it raises your heart rate and speeds up your breathing. You don't have to get your hour of exercise all at once—you can break it up throughout the day. How do you know if your body is working hard enough? Here's a good rule of thumb: When you're exercising or playing, if you're breathing too hard to sing but you can talk fairly easily, you're going at a good pace.

Just remember that whatever type of exercise you choose, don't get too hung up on counting minutes or monitoring your heart rate. The most important thing is to find fun activities that you love and to do them often.

It Adds Up

Do you take the escalator when you could climb the stairs? Do you beg for a ride when you're going only a couple of blocks? A few simple changes to your daily routine can make a difference.

- Ride your bike to the library instead of taking the bus.
- Volunteer for muscle-building chores, such as weeding the garden or raking leaves.
- Play a game of tag with your little sister or brother.
- Take the dog for a long walk.

S-T-R-E-T-C-H

Follow these stretching secrets to help prevent injuries and to build strength and flexibility.

- *Stretch slowly.* No matter how excited you are to get into the game or back to the locker room, don't rush. The whole point is to ease your muscles carefully into or out of your workout, and that takes time.

- *Don't bounce.* Bobbing up and down can damage your muscles. Once you strike your stretching position, stay there.

- *Hold it!* Try to hold your stretch for a count of at least ten to be sure your muscles get the message. Don't forget to breathe!

- *Stretch both sides.* When limbering up your arms, legs, waist, or neck, be sure to give equal time to the front, back, left, and right.

Sports Safety

Even the best athletes can get injured. Play it smart! These simple strategies will help you stay in the game.

Warm Up, Cool Down

Whether you're hiking, biking, or spiking a volleyball, always take time to stretch out your muscles and prepare them for the work they're about to do. A proper warm-up eases your body into gear and helps prevent muscle pulls and tears. At the end of your workout, cool down with more gentle stretching. This reduces stiffness and soreness the next day.

Concussions

Think of a concussion as a bruise inside your brain—there is a little bit of swelling and aching. Compared to other parts of the body, your brain—the control center of your body—heals differently. Concussions take time to get better, and if you don't give yourself a break, then the injury will just stick around longer. Give your brain a rest after a concussion, and stay off screens, because using devices will slow healing.

All concussions are different: Some are more serious than others, and the symptoms can vary from person to person. It's important to have your doctor check you out if you have a concussion. People with a concussion can have a headache, lack coordination, feel nauseated, experience sleepiness, feel confused, and have a whole host of other symptoms. It's important for you and your parents and coaches to know the signs of concussion. When in doubt, sit it out. Never go back to a game when you think you have a concussion.

Wear the Right Gear

You already know how important it is to wear your helmet when biking, inline skating, skateboarding, or skiing. But it might not occur to you to wear bright clothes so others can see you coming! And don't head out on skates without elbow, wrist, and knee guards. Other sports might call for a mouth guard or special padding—check with your coach to see what's recommended. Always wear shoes and clothing that fit properly. High-tops that don't fit snugly can lead to twisted ankles. Skates that are too small are an invitation for blisters.

Don't Overdo It

Pay attention to how your body feels while you're exercising or playing a sport. If you are in pain, are getting dizzy or sick to your stomach, or are unable to catch your breath, stop immediately and rest. All of these are warning signs to s-l-o-o-o-w down.

Drink LOTS of Water

When you're active, your body keeps cool by producing sweat. You need to replace the fluids your body is losing by drinking lots of water before, during, and after exercising. Fill up a sports bottle before you get going, and refill it often.

Sprain Training

Whether you're a ballet dancer or a soccer goalie, you'll probably deal with an injury at some point. One of the most common injuries is a *sprain*, a painful pull or tear in the tissue of a joint that causes the joint to swell up and turn black and blue. Fingers, wrists, elbows, knees, and ankles are easy targets. If you think you've sprained something, follow the first-aid rules of RICE, as shown below. If you are in a lot of pain or not getting better, then get to a doctor as soon as you can to get checked out.

Rest. Avoid using the sprained joint or putting weight on it.

Ice. Apply an ice pack—or bag of frozen peas or corn—to help shrink swelling and ease the pain.

Compression. Wrap the sprained area snugly in a stretchy sports bandage to stabilize it and to protect it from further injury.

Elevation. Keep the sprained joint raised on a couple of pillows to help the swelling go down.

Rest

To be healthy, you need plenty of rest. Sleep is your body's way of recharging to meet the challenges of each new day.

Good Night!

What's the secret to a sound night's sleep? Develop good sleeping habits. Getting enough rest helps you feel your very best.

Stick to a regular bedtime. One of the best ways to ensure a good night's sleep is to get up and go to bed at the same time every day. If you sleep late one morning, then get up early the next, you may feel tired and groggy all day and have trouble sleeping that night.

Develop a routine. It's a good idea to create a *ritual*, a special routine, that tells your body it's time to go to sleep. Listen to gentle music, take a warm bath, read a book, or write in a journal. Try to repeat your ritual every night at the same time.

Exercise. Active girls who exercise regularly are often the soundest sleepers of all. Exercise helps release extra energy and tension that can interfere with sleep. But don't exercise too close to bedtime or you might have trouble winding down!

Watch what you drink. Many sodas—especially colas—contain *caffeine*, which can make you feel jumpy and wide awake. Caffeine is also in coffee, tea, and chocolate. Avoid anything with caffeine at night, especially close to bedtime.

Don't go to bed stuffed. A tummy that's churning because it's too full makes a bad bunkmate. If your stomach is growling from hunger, grab a light snack.

How Many ZZZs?
Some girls need more sleep than others, but most girls your age need at least ten hours of sleep per night. When your body is growing and changing, you may need more sleep than usual. Aim to get the same amount of sleep each night to give your body consistency—this is the very best way to stay healthy and to grow well. But if you have a few nights in a row of staying up late and you feel exhausted, try catching up on the weekend by going to bed early, sleeping in, or taking a nap.

Sleep Troubles

Do you dread going to bed? Is nighttime a nightmare for you? Lots of girls have problems that creep into their sleep.

Bed-Wetting

Wetting the bed is a condition that doctors call *enuresis* (en-yer-EE-sis), and it's more common than you might think. Enuresis usually occurs when a person's bladder is too small to hold all the urine her body produces in the night. If the sleeper doesn't wake up in time to go to the bathroom, she wets the bed. Almost everyone with this condition outgrows it eventually—and usually if a girl has it, one of her parents did, too. If you're struggling with enuresis, talk to your health care provider; she might have additional treatment options.

Insomnia

"I've got *insomnia*" is a fancy way of saying "I can't sleep." Insomnia is often caused by having a lot on your mind. You may be so excited or worried about something that you can't stop thinking about it. Insomnia can also be caused by caffeine and other chemicals in certain foods and medicines. Almost everyone has insomnia once in a while, but if you find yourself wide awake night after night, talk to a parent or your doctor. In the meantime, try this relaxation trick. Close your eyes and lie on your back. Then relax your feet, relax your legs, and keep going until you've relaxed every muscle in your body. From head to toe, you'll be ready to go—straight to sleep, that is!

To unwind your mind, try listening to relaxing music or to recordings of soothing sounds from nature.

Nightmares

It's normal to have a bad dream occasionally. Nightmares can seem very realistic, or they can make no sense at all. Either way, they're usually related to something real that's bothering you. If scary dreams invade your sleep every night, talk to your parents or a counselor to help you find out what's on your mind.

Body Talk

It's hard to feel perky in the a.m. when you've got sleep problems that plague you in the p.m.!

Too Worried to Sleep

I have trouble sleeping. I try reading and relaxing before bed. My parents are getting a divorce, but I don't like thinking about it. It hurts! Do you think deep in my mind I think about the divorce and it's keeping me up?

Hurt & Sleepy

Emotional upset and anxiety can definitely cause sleepless nights. Of course you feel scared and sad about your parents' divorce—any girl would. But when your daytime worries start to haunt you at bedtime, you need to do more than toss and turn. You need to get help. Talk to your parents, a teacher, a counselor, or another adult you trust about how much you're hurting. It's hard to have sweet dreams when you've got a heavy heart.

Security Blanket

I am 11 years old and I still sleep with a "blankie." I know a lot of girls do, but definitely not as old as me! Every time I go to a friend's to sleep over, she says stuff like, "Did you bring your security blanket?" and then laughs her head off.

Still sleeping with a "blankie"

Have you considered taking just a piece of your bedtime buddy with you? Cut off a teeny corner of your blanket and pin it inside your sleeping bag—a secret place that only you know about. Or, if you can't bear to cut up your blanket, maybe you can laugh along with your friend. When she asks about the blanket, say with a smile, "You know me, I never leave home without it!" And don't worry, you'll give up your blanket when you're ready.

Bed Wetter

I still wet my bed. My best friend doesn't know and keeps inviting me to slumber parties. She feels sad when I say I can't go. I would really like to sleep over to make my friend happy, but how can I do it without getting embarrassed?

Ashamed

Keeping your bed-wetting a secret only adds to the feeling that it's something shameful—and it's not. If your friend is kind and caring, you may find there's relief in telling her the truth. You can still enjoy sleepovers with your friend by inviting her to your house. If she's having a party, ask if you can go to the first half of the party and have your parents pick you up before bedtime. You'll get to share in most of the fun. You're sure to outgrow bed-wetting eventually. But in the meantime, talk to your doctor about solutions.

Night Fright

I'm afraid of the dark and I can't sleep. What should I do?

afraid

For starters, you need to figure out exactly what it is about the dark that frightens you. Once you've identified what triggers your fright, ask your parents to help you brainstorm ways to banish your fears. Are there things in the room that scare you, such as the dark closet, the curtains flapping in the window, or other objects that cast scary shadows? Try placing a night-light in your room so that you can see in all the dark corners. Is it night noises that give you the heebie-jeebies? Investigate the source of the spooky sounds in the light of day. Once you know that *creak-creak* is coming from the furnace and not from phantoms, you're sure to rest easier.

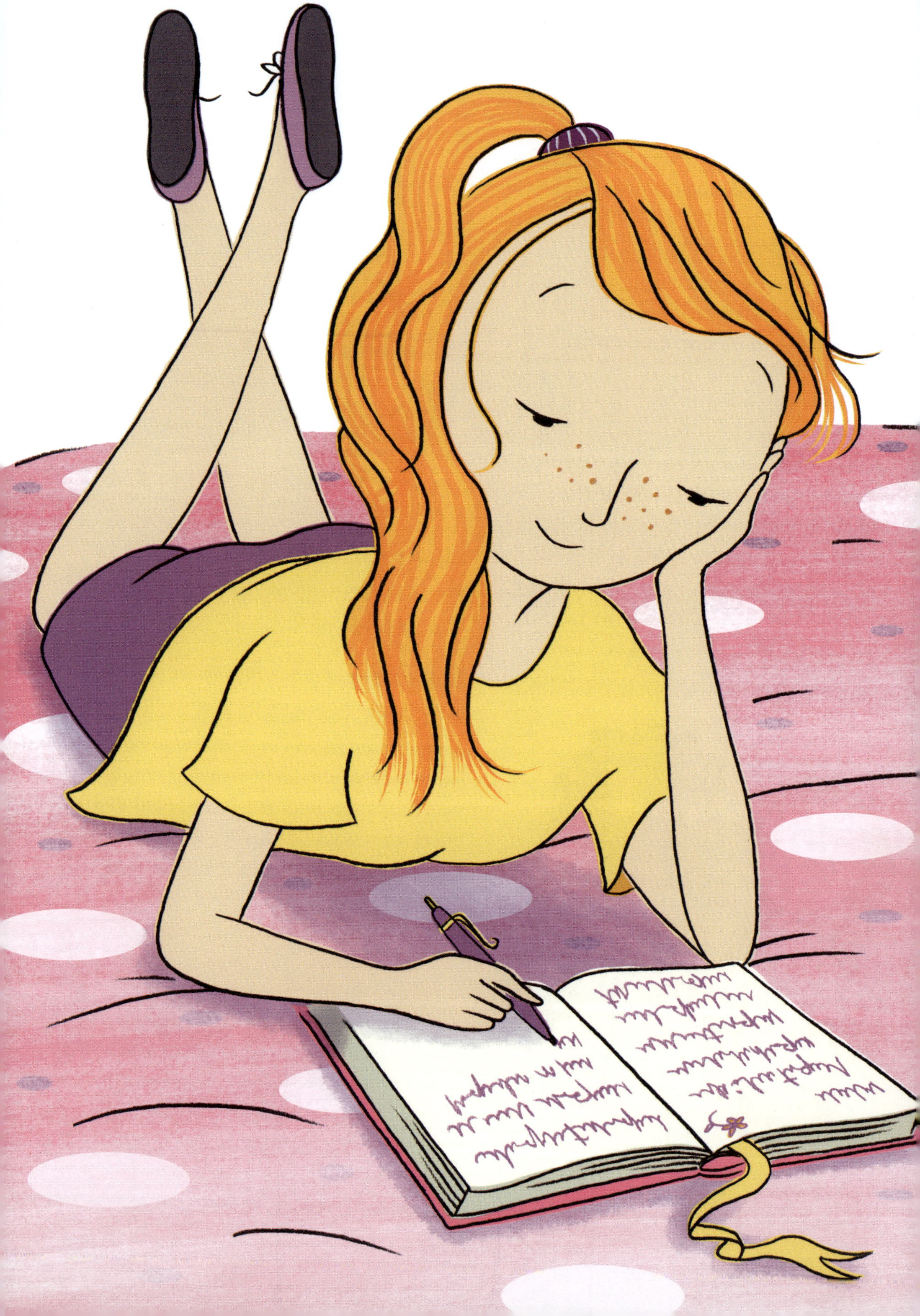

The Girl Inside

Taking care of your **feelings** is just as important as taking care of your body. Find out what to do when oceans of emotions are washing over you, and get tips for **talking it out** with family and friends. Finally, as you get ready to move forward into the future, take a moment to stop and celebrate **the whole you!**

Your Feelings

Mad one minute, sad the next? Feel like you're riding an emotional roller coaster? You're not mixed up, you're just growing up!

It's normal for a growing girl to want a little privacy. Just make sure that when you shut the bedroom door, you don't shut out the people you love. Puberty can be a confusing time, but it doesn't need to be a lonely one. Now more than ever, you need the support of your family.

Ups and Downs

You already know the outside of you will undergo big changes during puberty. But you might not be prepared for so many changes on the inside. During this time, it's normal to experience strong emotions. Don't be surprised if your moods come and go and change like the weather. One minute you're feeling sunny, the next minute stormy. What's behind this flood of laughter and tears? Hormones! The same hormones that tell your body to change and grow can strongly affect your feelings, too.

New Directions

As you get older, it's natural for your interests to change. Some of the toys and games you used to love suddenly get pushed to the back of the closet. New interests may take their place. You might start liking new music or a new sport or hobby that you've never tried before. That's perfectly OK. There's room in your life for lots of different interests, old and new.

Hang On

It's easy to get caught up in the tide of what other girls are saying and doing. They may even put pressure on you to do as they do. But be careful. Try not to get lost in the crowd and lose sight of what's right for you. If your friends are super into movie stars and makeup and you'd rather be building a tree fort, don't just cave in and go with the flow. Listen to your heart and be true to you.

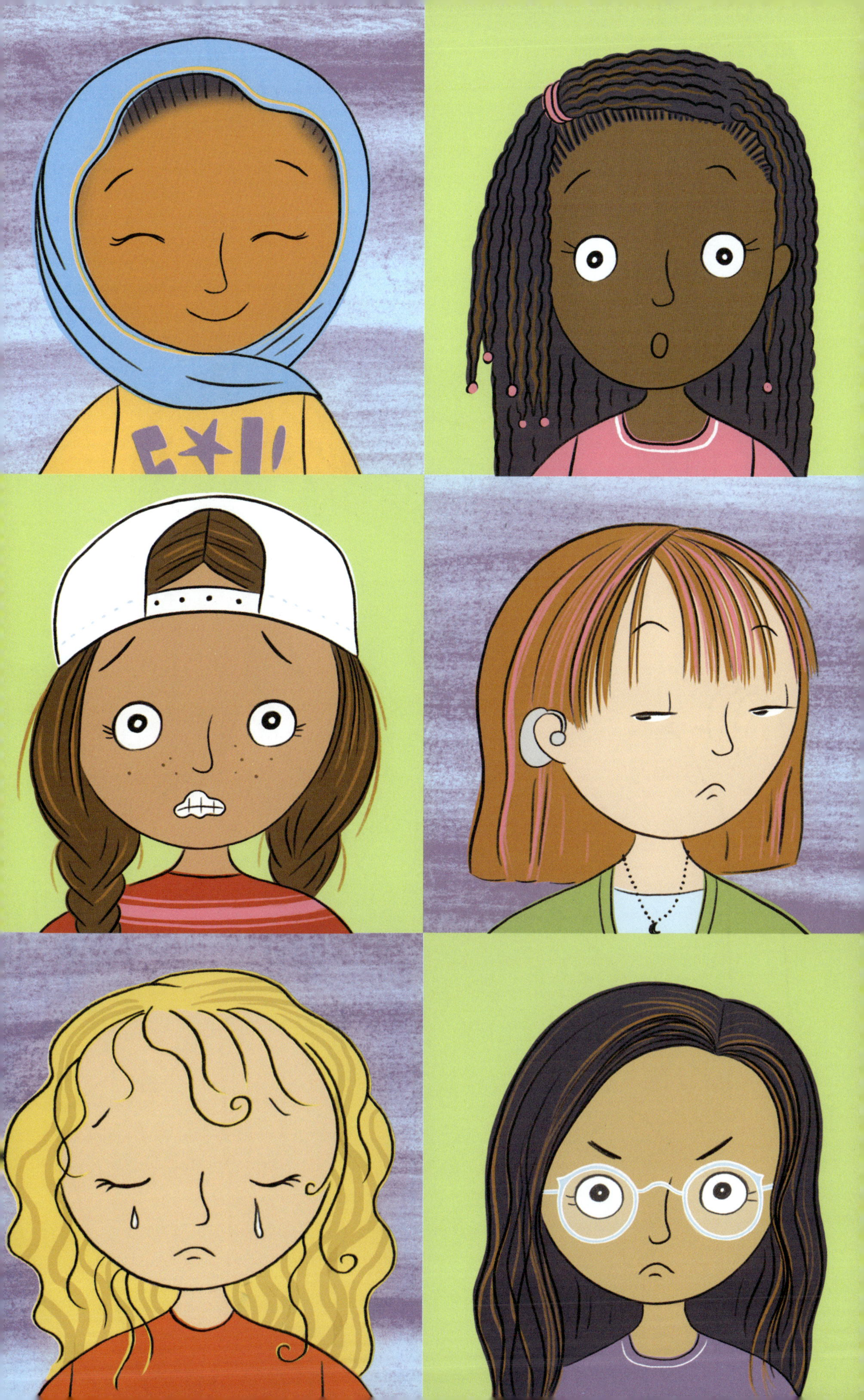

Time Out!

Tantrums are expected for two-year-olds, who don't know how to control their emotions. But tears and screaming won't get you what you want now that you're older. Part of growing up is learning how to express anger and frustration calmly, in a way that's fair to others.

"It's good to talk out problems with the people you have them with." —Ukiah

Dealing with Feelings

"Forget it. You won't understand."
"You treat me like a baby!"
"I hate you!"

Your whole world is turned topsy-turvy, and there's a tidal wave of emotion crashing around inside you. You might feel angry, jealous, afraid, embarrassed, or just plain lost and confused. What do you do? If you're like many people, you take it out on the people closest to you. And the trouble with this is that sulky silences and angry outbursts build a wall between people. The wall doesn't go up overnight—it's built one brick at a time. A mean word here. A slammed door there. Before you know it, there's a wall too high for either side to climb over. Don't let this happen. Instead of building walls, build bridges by learning to say how you feel in a healthy, helpful way.

Cooling Down

Before you can talk about your feelings, you need to have a calm head. Take a few deep breaths. Go for a walk. Take a bath. Write in your journal. Cuddle the dog. Blow off steam, and you'll be less likely to say or do something that you'll regret later. Once you've cooled down, you're ready to talk.

Talking It Out

Telling people how you feel, honestly and calmly, can bring you closer. It shows that you trust them with your feelings. And you open the door for them to share their feelings with you. Besides, talking to others can help you sort out confusing feelings. You need to be able to share anger, fear, and sadness—as well as excitement and happiness—to get the support you need during this challenging time.

Making It Better

Anger can be helpful when it leads to change. For that to happen, you need to try to explain how you feel. Follow these steps to say what's on your mind:

1. Describe exactly what made you angry: "Mom, it made me mad when you said I couldn't have a new swimsuit, right off the bat, without even listening to my reasons for wanting one."

2. Tell how it made you feel: "I felt like you didn't care about my feelings."

3. Try to agree on a way to handle things in the future: "Next time, let's hear each other out before deciding. Maybe together we'll think of a solution that will make us both happy."

The Whole You

Always remember there's more—much more—to you than your body. It's your head, your heart, and your spirit, too, that add up to make YOU.

You have a unique way of **seeing** the world.

You **listen** to other points of view.

You are ready to **reach** out to others.

Your head is abuzz with creative ideas, hopes, and **dreams.**

You confidently **express** your thoughts and feelings.

Your heart is full of **kindness.**

You **speak out** and **stand up** for what's right.

You're ready to **move ahead** to a bright future!

Write to us!

At American Girl, we love hearing from girls just like you. Tell us what you think of *The Care & Keeping of You 1*. Send your thoughts and questions to:

The Care & Keeping of You 1 Editor
American Girl
2330 Eagle Drive
Middleton, WI 53562

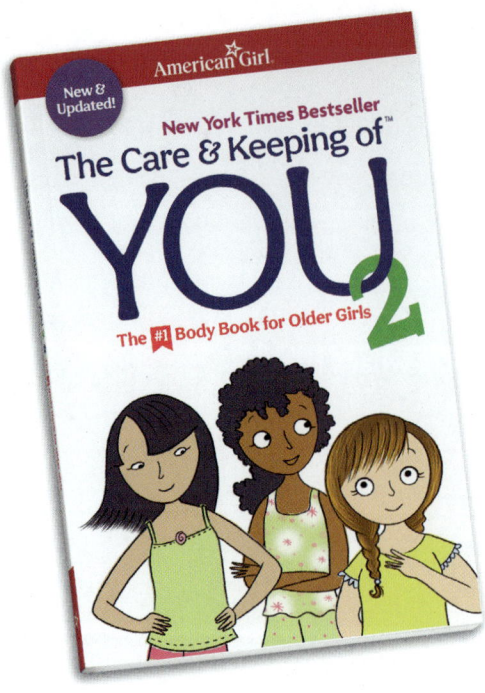

(All comments and suggestions received by American Girl may be used without compensation or acknowledgment. Sorry—photos can't be returned.)

Comfortable with the information you read in this book? If so, great! Understanding your changing body and feelings is an important part of growing up. What you learned may be enough for now, but soon, as you continue to develop, you might have more questions and need more advice. When you do, *The Care & Keeping of You 2* will be waiting for you!

Each sold separately. Find more books online at americangirl.com.

americangirl.com/play

Discover online games, quizzes, activities, and more at **americangirl.com/play**